YOUNG WIDOW

Learning to Live Again

KATE CONVISSOR

ZondervanPublishingHouse
Grand Rapids, Michigan

A Division of HarperCollins*Publishers*

Requests for information should be addressed to:
Zondervan Publishing House
Grand Rapids, Michigan 49530

Library of Congress Cataloging-in-Publication Data

Convissor, Kate.
    Young widow : learning to live again / Kate Convissor
        p. cm.
    ISBN 0-310-54941-8 (paper)
    1. Widows—United States. 2. Widowhood—United States.
    3. Widows—United States—Religious life. I. Title.
HQ1058.5.U5C66   1992
306.88—dc20   92–14869
                                                                    CIP

Edited by Lori J. Walburg
Cover designed by Ron Kadrmas

Printed in the United States of America

92 93 94 95 96 97 / CH / 10 9 8 7 6 5 4 3 2 1

*To Richard,
who showed me butterflies*

*To Craig,
who showed me crystal rainbows
and nightcrawlers*

Contents

Acknowledgments   9

Introduction   *11*

Grieving Alone

1. The Journey Begins   *17*
   My husband is dead

2. Before the Beginning   *25*
   My preparation for widowhood

3. Like a Butterfly   *31*
   Glimpses of the resurrection

4. Summer of Shaky Knees   *37*
   My first months alone

Sisters in Grief

5. Facing Forever   *47*
   What we have lost

6. Last Days   *55*
   The nature of his death

7. Light Through the Curtain   *61*
   The pitfalls and progress of grief

8. Fellowship of Love   *75*
   Suffering unites

9. Why?   *83*
   Faith sustains

Children of Grief

10. Death and the Children   91
        Healing the little ones
11. Families in Flux   105
        Surviving adolescence; forming new families

Moving On

12. The Turning   *121*
        The process of uncoupling
13. Woman Alone   *131*
        Deciding to move on
14. And Then There Are Men   *137*
        Deciding to date
15. Father of Waters   *149*
        God responds to the unanswerable
16. The Harvest   *157*
        New life begins

Epilogue   *165*

Appendix A   *166*
        A Note to the Helpers

Appendix B   *171*
        National Groups for the Widowed

Appendix C   *172*
        Suggested Reading

Notes   *174*

Acknowledgments

First, my family. A special hug for my parents, Jean and Ted Selby, who have always stood behind me without intruding on my life. And to Mildred Cesarz-Jenkins, for her courage and good example, and to my great sisters and brothers: Shawn, Chiara, Cindy, Mark, Rebecca, Scott, Diane, and Doug.

And thanks to the others who have been family to me: Dee Burkel and Jan Coffman, special sisters; the people of St. Mary's Parish in Chelsea for such amazing support and generosity; the deacons of the Lansing Diocese; Margaret Convissor; Bishop Kenneth Povish; Fr. Philip DuPuis; and the Chelsea Ministerial Fellowship. Thanks also to Ben Lockerd, Sandy Vander Zicht, and Lori Walburg for their warmth, encouragement, and editorial help.

Finally, a special thanks to the women who shared their stories with me. Their names have been changed, but their candor, tears, courage, and humor have put flesh on the bones of this book.

Introduction

The roadside park was lush and green, a solitary gem hidden among the trees. Drawn by its emerald splendor, I stopped to read and rest a bit.

What a treat just to be alone! I had with me only a small duffel bag, no carseats, diaper bags, bottles, or toys. My four little ones were home with their dad, and this was my weekend off. The freedom was heady. I felt young and alive.

Seated at a shady table, I listened while the pine and maple tossed summer secrets back and forth. Then I reached for my Bible and flipped it open. There had been little enough time, lately, to listen to God. I wanted to start this weekend right.

But the words that leapt from the open page were stark and unexpected, a harsh contrast to the exuberant beauty of the summer day.

> *Naked I came from my mother's womb,*
> *and naked I will depart.*
> *The LORD gave and the LORD has taken away;*
> *may the name of the LORD be praised. (Job 1:21)*

Startling as this passage was, it touched me. *Why this, Lord?* I asked. *Why does it move me so? Is it the yieldedness, Job's stalwart trust in the face of such great trouble? Could I ever be that supple in your hands?*

That day began my apprenticeship, a treacherous

journey toward Job-like trust. I had found the first rose blooming at the threshold of the desert.

In the years following, I would encounter death through my husband's ministry as a full-time deacon in our parish. I witnessed death's randomness as loved ones were unexpectedly snatched away. I saw its sloth as, week after week, Richard visited those whose bodies were consumed by inches while their families waited in helpless agony.

I knew as I watched that I could never fathom humankind's anguished "Why?" Death's purpose is inscrutable and its disturbing riddle better left with the one who first composed it. "I'll never question God," I told myself.

Then, when death encircled me, when I studied my husband's face in his coffin while our child, our fifth child, waited to be born, then I learned of God. At the time of my widowhood when my need was desperate, I learned that grace was enough.

How simple that sounds! But when you live each day stretched to the edge of physical and emotional endurance, it is everything. It is the miracle of wandering in a barren desert and of finding, not only clear, life-giving water, but roses blooming at its edge.

With death as my midwife and grief my baptism, I have seen the desert bloom. I am a different person now. I have survived. I have grown, and so have my children. That is God's work in me; it is mine to tell. This story is my psalm.

But the roses aren't mine. They are for your desert journeying. With the telling of the story, one last time, I catch their scent. I remember struggle and tears, pain and victory. A hardy strain, these roses thrive in salt and arid waste. I hope that they will be as fragrant and encouraging for you as they were for me.

And a last word of clarification. Richard was an ordained deacon in the Roman Catholic Church, one of the few deacons who worked full-time in the church. Like all deacons, he preached, married, and baptized, among many other duties. While I remain rooted in my tradition, this story is "catholic" in its best sense, meaning universal. There are no ideological boundaries to death or mourning, or to the grace that transfigures them.

When some beloved voice that was to you
Both sound and sweetness, faileth suddenly,
And silence against which you dare not cry,
Aches round you like a strong disease and new—
What hope? What help? What music will undo
That silence to your sense? Not friendship's sigh,
Nor reason's subtle count. . . .
Nay, none of these,
Speak Thou, availing Christ!—and fill this pause.

—Elizabeth Barrett Browning, "Substitution"

Grieving Alone

1

The Journey Begins
My husband is dead

I heard the wind that day in March, saw it toss trees and gently arch telephone wires. The wind blew from the west as it does every spring, buffeting my house of bricks, which always stood so firm against it. In this blue-water state, I've seen the springtime winds whip the inland lakes into turbulent froth. But I'd never seen the "Big Lake," as those who live on its shores call it.

To the west, the Big Lake—Lake Michigan—dwarfs all others in size and temperament. Wind and storm blow suddenly from the west. "The swells come from nowhere, sometimes fifteen feet high," they told me later. But I didn't know. Cradled in the center of the state, I'd never seen the Big Lake.

Through the kitchen window, I could see the cherry

and evergreen trees I'd planted, the lavender and sage that flourished in my bedraggled herb garden. This was my favorite view as I went about kitchen tasks; I'd often pause at the window, full of contentment. I felt happy and loved.

Life was good just then—predictable enough to be secure, dynamic enough to be challenging. I had a good marriage built on years of committed effort. And I had good kids, four of them, and one on the way.

My husband, Richard, had grown in his five years as a minister in our church. He had become valued and skilled in his work. His rough edges had been scoured, and a softer compassion and wisdom had matured him. Parishioners sought him out with the confusions and difficulties of their lives.

Still looking out the kitchen window, I was startled to see the state police car pull up outside. I hoped the children, just home from school, hadn't noticed—the raw authority, the badge and gun, might frighten and confuse them.

"Afternoon, ma'am. I just need to know if your husband's home."

"No, he's up fishing near Lake Michigan. Why?"

Why? Why? Why? I screamed inside.

"Well, his car's been found parked by the lake, but we haven't located him yet. I just have to verify that he actually is up there and that it is his car."

Relief flooded me. "Is that all? Yes, he's there, but he often fishes the rivers and nearby lakes, so he could be camping somewhere else. What's the concern? Has the car been there long?"

The officer avoided my eyes. "Well, a fisherman was washed off the Elberta Pier into the lake. An elderly couple saw it happen and reported it to the police. Divers are out in the lake, but nothing's been found so far."

Fear ran icy fingers across my scalp. My life had been so sheltered. Close calls and minor emergencies had always dwindled into nothing. This was the big one. But maybe it would still be nothing. Maybe he was just fishing somewhere else. Maybe.

Outside time, I waited for news of life or death. Would I breathe a sigh of relief and quickly return to normal? Or would I face an incomprehensible jolt and ragged turn that would lead—where? I waited for an eternity, like all the women who have waited before me, eyes fixed on far horizons for a mast, a cloud of dust, any reassurance that our men are coming home. We bathe the children, we tidy the house, we go on as the rising dread catches in our throats.

The kids watched TV early that night as I paced, wanting to be alone, to prepare . . . for what? Of course he'd come back. He always did. Only forty-five, Richard was a risk-taker, full of restless vitality, always pressing his limits, and always squeaking through somehow.

I remembered a dream I'd had a few months earlier. So vividly I dreamed of his death. I saw myself at his funeral and felt a fierce determination to survive with courage and dignity. The intensity of that dream had lingered into the next day, long after he'd come home.

"Dear God," I prayed now. "Let this cup pass from me. I don't want to drink it."

The police car pulled up again outside the window; the same officer's face was taut with the difficulty of his task. "It was your husband," he said. Quick and blunt. I was grateful for the clean cut.

How do you tell your children that their father is dead? How do you so brutally smash the security of their lives? The four small bodies pressed around me for animal comfort as we sat together on the couch. We did not yet understand. Then I called our friend John, the funeral director, and the world surged in.

I suppose a man's funeral captures the essence of his life. Richard's gift was unflinching acceptance. He embraced humanity with forthright honesty, no matter if you were prince or pauper, lovely or leprous. "He had a way of coming in the kitchen door while everyone else was banging on the front," a friend said, tears running down his face.

While he worked at the church, I wondered in my secret heart how he would ever gain the political support he needed if he spent so much time with the powerless— the elderly, the ill, and the homebound. Although our purpose is to serve these small ones, they generally have no voice in parish matters, and certainly no finger on the purse strings.

"Jim loves to fish," Richard said one day. "I'm taking him out fishing tomorrow while he can still make it." Later, Richard offhandedly described how he'd carried the young man dying of leukemia to the boat, where they had spent the afternoon fishing. Some time later he drove to Detroit for the lengthy, arduous process of having platelets removed from his blood to be given to Jim. To him it was no big deal. It was just a day's work.

In the days preceding his funeral, I learned about my husband from the stories and memories of the people he'd touched. Hundreds of friends, some I hadn't seen in a decade, streamed through the funeral home and filled the church. Their open grief and the memories they shared were more precious to me than flowery words and promises.

Now it was my turn to occupy the front pew I'd seen so many others fill. I prayed for dignity—just to get through this final day without breaking down. I'd chosen the songs and Scripture for the funeral service. I'd borrowed clothes to fit my seven-month belly. I'd made all the decisions with numb efficiency: a casket made of oak, strong and deeply-rooted like Richard; a secluded gravesite under a tall evergreen that we could visit in privacy; a burial suit and the stole symbolic of his ministry; and another pair of glasses to replace those that lay at the bottom of the lake.

The people of my parish worked doggedly to prepare for this last day. I just needed to get through it. *And please, Lord,* I prayed, *make little Luke sit still during the funeral service so I can pay attention.*

I was grateful for the full church, for the deacons and priests lining the altar with their white robes. I was grateful for my pastor's grief and my bishop's presence, all memories I would keep, just as I had pressed the autumn asters from our wedding a dozen years before. I absorbed the graceful ritual without inner or outer distraction while Luke scribbled intently beside me with a scrap of paper and a pencil stub.

The "Ode to Joy," full-throated and triumphant, swept us out the door to the chill embrace of silence and gray skies. A deep quiet comes with the grave; even grief stands mute. I remembered this silence from my little brother's funeral: the chill, the creaking pulleys that lowered his coffin, our still figures huddled against a wide, slate sky. A hushed, measured beat, death marches always forward, marking time. No turning back.

As my husband's coffin entered the earth, a scrap of paper fluttered onto its lid—Luke's gift to a father he'd known so briefly. "I love you, Dad," he'd written in child-scrawl.

I embraced the silence, craved it. I wanted to be still for a long time, to heal and ponder this incomprehensible thing that had happened, to rant and shake my fist at God if need be. This was a pain so profound that the tears, the numbness, the disbelief, were all ripples on the surface of a deep, black pool of water. Nothing disturbed its depths. It seemed a well from which grief emanated, a core of my being I had reached only through extreme tribulation.

Yet I had children to raise who were as shaken and hurt as I, and a new baby coming. That lonely birth loomed ahead, a treacherous slope.

After two weeks, the kids were ready to return to school from sheer boredom. Relatives went home, and I resumed an unthinking housekeeping routine.

Little Luke proudly occupied his dad's empty place at the table as we sniffled through our first meal alone. "I can tell when you've been crying," said nine-year-old Naomi, running for the tissue box. "Your nose turns red." The box of tissues went round with the bowl of beans, and I'm not sure which was emptied first.

In a burst of energy, I tore the house apart that Easter, moving bed rails over the heads of startled guests, clearing a spot in my room for the baby. Might as well do the heavy work while men were around.

That was the nature of my grief, to hurry it up. Feel the pain and get it over with. I gave away Richard's clothes, clutching at the familiar smell and feel of that old sweater, this gray herringbone jacket.

I saved his wallet, still molded to the shape of his

pocket. He could pull the most amazing things from that wallet—phone numbers and memorabilia from years gone by. I emptied his junk drawer, which, like every man's, held his special stones and pennies—the same treasures I'm sure he pocketed as a boy. Again I breathed his closeness, the small change of his life.

I took off my wedding ring very soon. It was uncomfortable to wear the symbol of a life that was no longer. Smooth from years of wear, its spot indented on my finger, the ring resisted being laid aside. My finger bore its mark for some time. I reached for it sometimes out of habit and was always startled to find it gone.

In some ways I had no choice but to hurry on. Self-pity and depression were indulgences my children would pay for. They tugged at me with the physical burden of their care, with worry over the emotional wounds they carried, with years of financial support to provide.

I didn't know the best way through such a tempest, but I found I could trust my instincts; I knew what was good for me. Like a physical wound that seeps and bleeds, the spirit also struggles to heal. I felt wounded, an amputee; even my appearance felt different. A wound heals slowly from the inside out; some never heal completely, and all grievous wounds leave scars.

One thing I knew with certainty: I had begun a grueling journey, one I might not survive without a massive infusion of grace. Without God, some part of me might die. This very clarity was a grace; I was poised on the brink of a mortal test, a great experiment. Were God's promises true and would they be enough?

I had no choice but to go forward in blind trust.

2

Before the Beginning
My preparation for widowhood

Of course I was unprepared to be a widow. We had no will, few savings, and haphazard financial planning. Even in these liberated times, my husband had worked, and I had borne children and kept house. I'd chosen to stay home and adjusted over the years to a housewife's isolation and transparent social position. I had no job skills, no paycheck, no identity of my own.

In her book *The Hiding Place*, Corrie ten Boom tells the story of a loving father who gives his child a ticket to board the train at just the right time, not too soon lest the ticket is lost or so late the train is missed. When my time came to make this journey, God had given me the ticket. In unforeseen ways over many years, he had prepared me.

Boot camp was the Detroit ghetto. Young and

altruistic, I came to Detroit in 1970 to attend college—and survived a far more rigorous schooling. Extremes of humanity struggle in the city, extremes of degradation and dignity, of evil and crystalline goodness. Any breath of beauty—sunset splashed against the buildings or a smile on a stranger's face—shines radiant amid the squalor and poverty of the city streets.

The city taught me that God is faithful. I walked the alleys unharmed and became acquainted with its peoples: the old men who gather trash, the small children who play there. I did my laundry on the hookers' corner, observing the joyless women who sold their bodies and the men who bought them. I moved within this world unobtrusively, learning and being stretched by it but protected from its creeping desperation.

Our little church perched on the edge of the expressway, a medieval remnant of stone and stained glass. Within its sanctuary a motley piecework of mankind found shelter. Some of us, young students at the university, began reaching out to the war-torn community around us.

We visited some of the halfway houses which saturated the neighborhoods. Hundreds of former mental patients lived a twilight death in these houses. Sitting among the unwashed and insane in dark houses that smelled of urine, I was quickly cleansed of any smug film of Christian condescension.

During one visit I joined a circle of women who drooped like wilted flowers around the dining room table. Deaf to my nervous chatter, they waited, slumped and immobile, for the next meal. The same chilling lethargy began creeping over me. Silent now, I sat among my Stonehenge sisters absorbing their experience: the stale cigarettes and old coffee, the mildewy dampness. For one transcendent moment I was no longer the visitor, separate and above. I was one of them.

I'll never comprehend the quirks of chemistry and weight of sorrow that brought them to that place. But while I was there I felt the fragile barriers of social class, education, mental stability. We build these walls thick and strong to protect our own frailty. More broken now, I share their remnant places. My own walls are chinked, my soft places more exposed.

Richard became a member of that church and we married in the city, living for a while unconventionally. Richard took a year-long leave of absence from his engineering job to work in our little parish, and I finally finished my degree as my belly grew with our first child. Friends and relatives filled our grand old home, reminiscent of bygone splendor with its French doors, broad mahogany-and-tile fireplace, and cramped servant's quarters.

But children tug us insistently toward stability and convention. Expecting our second child, we had little left to give the city and our family needed a new environment, one that demanded less struggle. We moved to a small town near Richard's new job, where the seasons passed effortlessly. I lost the constant alertness and quenched the confrontational style I had acquired in the city.

Peaceful years followed, when babies came as regularly as utility bills and I had no time to listen very closely to God. Yet the lesson I had learned in the city nestled in a corner of my mind: "God is faithful. Don't be afraid."

Middle age is a peculiar passage. Its crossing makes people restless and discontented. Turning thirty created some small turbulence for me. Who am I, anyway, besides somebody's wife and four somebodies' mom? What were those dreams I'd cherished? What do I want for my life now? What will I do when the kids are grown?

After a brief stint in a custom sewing business with two close friends, I reclaimed a childhood dream. Turning in my needle for a pencil and tape recorder, I cast off my natural timidity and hit the bricks as a freelance journalist. This new direction stretched my talents and my marriage, but in three years I had enough business to pay for my computer.

It was my best investment in the future. This talent was mine. When all the familiar boundaries had tumbled down, when my confidence drifted away like autumn leaves and I was suddenly the sole provider, a frail yet tenacious hope whispered, "You did it once, you can do it again."

But it was Richard, finally, who taught me about death.

A minister enters people's lives at their crossroads, at times of joy and sorrow, at beginnings and endings. As he grew in skill and compassion Richard was invited and sometimes begged to come into the private chambers of parishioners' lives. His daily contact with struggle and hurt put my own life in perspective.

"I'm depressed," I half-joked to Richard one day. "The kids have been fighting constantly, and I've gotten another rejection in the mail." But Richard didn't seem to hear. His eyes wandered to the wall behind me.

"I visited a lady today," he began slowly while I fidgeted. "She is losing both legs to diabetes, bit by bit.

Her circulation is so bad that they won't heal and keep getting reinfected. She's in a lot of pain."

His eyes penetrated mine. "You're not depressed," he said. "You're just feeling sorry for yourself."

Through him I saw the careening jolts a life can take, ending with swift and premature brutality, or dribbling away in a mist of pain and confusion. Life isn't fair and it isn't easy. Often it doesn't even make sense.

> "For my thoughts are not your thoughts,
> neither are your ways my ways,"
>   declares the LORD.
> "As the heavens are higher than the earth,
> so are my ways higher than your ways
> and my thoughts than your thoughts."
>   (Isaiah 55:8–9)

As my vision of God expanded over the years, so did my conviction that he orders things in ways I can't comprehend. But he orders them nonetheless. My work and my salvation are to accept, trust, love—such soft words, yet so dearly bought. What constant vigilance it takes to allow anger and doubt to pass over and through you without lodging in a crevice of your soul; what hard work to trust when there is every reason to doubt.

Through Richard's ministry I observed and pondered these things, and when death entered my house a foundation had been laid. I heard God's firm voice: "Now. Now, son, it is time for you to die." Like a child I envisioned that God was in the wave that took Richard, that some bit of the Eternal dwelled within the water, even as I repeatedly imagined the terror of Richard's last moments. I rejected the apparent randomness of this death. From the beginning I felt it was an act of finality, a purposeful consummation.

Death, governed by the Galaxy-walker, is the far horizon that illuminates life's day. Nor am I its helpless victim. I have choices: grow or be stunted, trust or withdraw in bitterness, live or let my spirit die.

A green stick before eternity, I am bent in the posture of Job. The hand of God has touched my life. Who am I to question his will?

Yet, frail imperfect flesh, I questioned. In the months that followed I argued with my husband: "Why did you leave me? Why so careless with your life?" My mind was divided, partly accepting the act of God, partly resisting the human flaw.

God waited patiently through these months of anger until, over a year later, he firmly repeated the lesson of his sovereignty.

3

Like a Butterfly
Glimpses of the resurrection

He *would* go. There was something single-minded about Richard. Set on a course, he had a crawdad's tenacious grip. When I met Richard his passion was photography. Every day after work he went out to take pictures in the afternoon light so prized by photographers. As shadows lengthened on the slums, he sought out its people.

"You gonna take my picture?" some would ask, posing.

"First tell me about yourself," he would say. And the stories would tumble out—prostitutes, addicts, children, all manner of humanity. "No, show me how you feel," he would urge. The posturing subject might go limp, broad smile fading, head drooping on hands. The children might turn cartwheels or do tricks. The alcoholic just lay unconscious in the weeds, a crutch and pair of bandaged legs the only sign of life.

He was tenacious about God and about his church. From the time of his conversion in his early thirties, Richard sought to know more about God and serve him better. An automotive engineer by training, he was led by a crooked course to the ministry. He had just completed a master's degree in theology the year before he died—a grueling three-year stint for all of us.

Fishing had become his latest obsession, as it had been for his father. Sometimes his fishing was a meditation, a silencing and gathering after a day of being spent. But I think the longer fishing trips simply tested his skill and endurance. Sometimes I resented the energy that went into these passions.

He knew I didn't want him to go this time. But it was early spring and the big lakes lure fishermen as surely as flies and spinners lure fish. Solicitous, he spent the evening at home, helping seven-year-old Esther with her First Communion project. She had several assignments to complete before receiving the sacrament. I could see that Richard had chosen one of the easiest that evening, and I was miffed. "Just trying to get away quicker," I sniffed.

"I'll be back late tomorrow," he said, brushing my cheek. Hurt and angry, I enjoyed the guilt in his eyes.

But our tomorrow never came. Eternity swept through the door, and the direction of our lives changed forever.

I sat in the front pew in church waiting for the memorial service to begin. Tomorrow was the funeral. On my right Richard lay in the coffin I had chosen. It was comforting to be so near him while greeting friends who stood patiently in a line stretching to the back of church.

Silent now, eyes closed, I let the quiet seep into my fatigue. I absorbed the rustling from the full church behind me, the dull ache in my back and legs. Despite hours of standing, despite my seven-month pregnancy, my ankles had not swollen at all. Then I smelled a spicy fragrance, elusive but insistent. What was it?

Lilies! From the floral arrangement on the altar, Easter lilies in white robes trumpeted their hope-filled song. Jesus is risen! Foolish ones, why look for him in the grave? Death is no more.

I could not take that step into rejoicing—death was looking pretty hale and hearty just then—but I welcomed the blessing of the lilies, those harbingers of resurrection, heralds of immortality.

I cannot imagine heaven. Yet, as humankind is made in the image of God, so his creation all around us must contain some scrap of Paradise. My eyes are just not clear enough.

Heaven may be very simple, like the children we must become in order to enter God's kingdom. It is the place for which we were made, "made for it stitch by stitch as a glove is made for a hand," says C. S. Lewis in *The Problem of Pain*.[1] Heaven is home in all its sweetness and warm security.

Someone I love, who shared my body and my mind, whose face I would recognize among a multitude, resides now in eternity. The ancient questions hover close. How is he? Where is he? *Who* is he now?

No answers come. Just the silent finger of faith, pointing. As I have without doubt known the love of God,

I entrust to him the eternity of my husband, and of everyone I love.

And as Richard taught me about death, he also pointed toward the resurrection.

"Just as a worm becomes a butterfly, death doesn't end life, only changes it," he had written in a funeral sermon.

That evening, after the memorial service, I lumbered upstairs to say good night to the kids. I had seen so little of them in the two days since Richard's death.

"How are you girls?" I asked, sitting on the bed.

We chatted about their day, the friends and the teachers who had come to the funeral home. But they had something else on their minds.

"Mom," said Esther, "I was thinking. Remember when we just found out that Dad died and everyone came over? Well, Mrs. Coffman was talking to us, and she said that now Dad is the butterfly and we are the caterpillars."

The image had gripped their imaginations. For two days they had pondered its significance and now were eager to discuss it.

"What does that mean to you girls?"

"It means that now Dad is free and beautiful," said Esther, her hands miming flight.

"Someday we'll be like that, too," said Naomi.

Eternity gently brushed my cheek, like wings. I touched the butterfly pinned to my collar. It was made of iridescent abalone shell rimmed in silver, a gift from a quick trip Richard had made to Florida just a few months before.

Tomorrow at the funeral I would wear the tiny gold butterfly with the pearl in the center. It had been a birthday present from him. Once the pearl had fallen out, and he had replaced it.

I said, "Did you girls know that your dad has given me three butterflies over the years? This pin and two necklaces. I've been wearing a different one each day since he died just to keep him near me."

Three butterflies. One for each of us. Although her dad wasn't there, Esther proudly wore the gold butterfly for her First Communion some weeks later.

I don't remember whether we ever got her projects done. I do remember shuffling through the papers that had drifted through the house like snowflakes after the funeral. Buried somewhere I found the project Richard had helped Esther with the night he left.

In precise block letters superimposed on wheat and grapes he had written: YOU SHALL LIVE FOREVER.

With butterflies and lilies I lay these treasures in memory's cupboard. Someday I won't need to wonder.

4

Summer of Shaky Knees
My first months alone

"You know I'm not very intuitive," my friend Dee said, breaking the silent prayer of the women's Bible study. "I don't see visions or anything, but just now I saw the Lord standing guard over you. Behind him were shadowy figures of things like anger and depression. His arms were outspread, holding them back and protecting you so nothing could harm you."

It was the week after Richard's funeral and I was on shaky, newborn legs. I was really too raw and unsteady to be out but had always enjoyed the common sense and strength of these women. I knew Dee's words were true. I felt that protection.

I had done what was necessary: contacted a lawyer, begun hundreds of thank-you notes, applied for Social

Security. Now there was just pain and all of life ahead. Pain, fierce and cleansing in its intensity, still without anger, guilt, or depression—all that would come later.

The grace I felt didn't blunt the pain, didn't even keep difficulties at bay. The cars still ran out of oil, fuses still blew, the grass needed mowing and our machine was too cantankerous for the job. These daily irritations were drips in an overflowing cup.

Grace was a sense of presence, of stillness, that was always there just below the surface. Perhaps grace had always been there, but my life had been too hurried, my mind too cluttered, to notice it. Perhaps a feeling of unworthiness had blocked the presence of God. All that fell away now. God was my Father, giving me each day the ticket for the journey, and I clung to that grace like a child.

The baby's birth was the next obstacle before my body and my life would be "normal" again. I dreaded that birth, a lonely, vulnerable time without the partner who had panted with me through all the others. I wanted it to be safely over, to begin rebuilding our lives.

Richard Stephen—"Stevie"—was born on a blistering May day, homely as usual but robustly sound. I had supremely skilled birthing companions in my mother and Dee, who had borne eighteen children between them, but it was a lonely delivery for me. I felt Richard's presence during the birth as I had a few times before, distinct but unreachable, off to my right.

The large city hospital was surprisingly sensitive to me. Several nurses gently but unobtrusively acknowledged that they knew this was a difficult time for me. Through administrative wizardry, I had no roommates in the semiprivate room that my insurance covered. I was spared the visits of someone else's proud papa, the murmuring of some other happy couple behind the curtain. I recall that kindness with deep gratitude.

While I lay in air-conditioned comfort, a crew of friends painted my bedrooms in the steamy heat while my mother and sister babysat cranky children. Everyone was working so hard to smooth the road for me. I was humbled by so much care.

Home again! Life steamrolled ahead. We had enough money from donations, Social Security, and life insurance to coast for a time, but I was driven to earn money and keep up my freelance contacts. I didn't want to lose sight of my career; after all, I was the breadwinner now, the sole provider for my children's education and my own security in old age. I was planning to be alone for a long time.

A month after Stephen's birth, my long-suffering baby-sitter was pacing through K-Mart with four little ones in tow while I did an interview nearby. The money I made was a pittance, but I drove myself relentlessly.

This was my summer of shaky knees, of living on the edge without a safety net. I was running on empty and hadn't even left the driveway. When we decided it was time for my mother to return to her own life a few weeks after Stephen's birth, I was alone. No back-up if I was sick, no one to watch the baby for ten minutes while I ran to the store. Only me to drive to swim meets and make every trivial decision. And my mind had molasses in the gears.

"Can I ride my bike downtown?" Uh, well, I didn't know. I guess so. Then all four kids were riding their bikes downtown, little Luke unsteadily peddling like fury to keep up. And I stood in a puddle of tears, aghast that I let it happen and terrified for their safety.

My emotions were on ice. "I'll think later," I kept telling myself. Later. Someday when the baby sleeps. When the kids go back to school. When the work is done. When I'm not so tired.

I couldn't talk, either. Couldn't joke or carry on an easy conversation as I used to. Once I asked a friend the same question three times, immediately forgetting both question and answer. At rare moments when the work was quelled and the kids in bed or occupied, I would sit and stare; my attention span couldn't even absorb a TV sitcom.

Doubt and anger began seeping into my mind. What if this wasn't God's will, but Richard's own recklessness or a random misfortune, without any greater significance than the death of the mosquito I swat on a summer's day?

In dreams, vivid and compelling, I tussled with the emotions that I squelched by day. I dreamed so vividly of Richard, his face and mannerisms perfectly in place. Sometimes he seemed loving but remote; other times we almost argued but not quite. When I woke, the familiar closeness left an empty ache in the harsh daylight.

During the day, memories stabbed me. A man jogging down the street looked like Richard. I missed the sloppy, sentimental "To My Loving Wife" cards I used to get on Mother's Day. I'd never get one of those again; I was nobody's wife. I drove by his office one night, saw light filtering softly through the curtains I'd made. In my mind's eye I could see the dust and clutter, the jerryrigged space heater and the slippers on the floor. He would never study there again.

But grace upheld me that long, hot summer. I felt it

in the release of tears and the love of my friends, in the incredibly stubborn health of my body and the whisper of Scripture.

> The Spirit of the Sovereign LORD is on me,
>   because the LORD has anointed me. . . .
> to comfort all who mourn,
>   and provide for those who grieve in Zion—
> to bestow on them a crown of beauty
>   instead of ashes,
> the oil of gladness
>   instead of mourning,
> and a garment of praise
>   instead of a spirit of despair.
> They will be called oaks of righteousness,
>   a planting of the LORD
>   for the display of his splendor.
>   (Isaiah 61:1–3)

Grace and my own natural stoicism made the forced march possible—and for that alone, I was grateful. I doggedly persisted, one eternal day at a time, only glancing sideways at the stark hardship of my life. I swallowed so much fear that summer that my throat hurt. How will we survive? Who will be a father to my children? What if the car breaks down? How will we get through Christmas?

I will not be afraid. Not be afraid. No, not afraid. I repeated my city-lesson like a mantra. Stand tall. Keep your shoulders back. Pay attention to your appearance. Let pain and fear wash over you; don't clutch against it. I was falling backwards in the dark and trusting God to catch me before I hit concrete.

Acceptance was the key, I knew. I needed to be like Mary and Job. Maybe I couldn't comprehend it all. Maybe

I could sense the first dark fingerlings of anger and doubt probing the edges of my mind. No matter. I tried to be aware of those feelings without letting them grab my throat. I tried to stay soft, accept myself, my feelings, and my lot in life. A verse by Dag Hammarskjold, the Swedish statesman, became my marching orders:

> For all that has been. Thanks.
> For all that will be. Yes.

One week that summer, all my children but the baby visited my parents. *Great,* I thought. *Finally some quiet in a house that will stay clean.* I laid the baby down, put on some Vivaldi, made tea, and wrapped up in soft, sweet silence.

My job was to empty Richard's office. I went through files of his work, the script as familiar as the way he walked, on his toes with that little bounce between steps. Here was his theology and Greek, notebooks full. Tough academic plowing for one not naturally bookish. His characteristic tenacity and the desire to grow filled those notebooks.

I listened to a tape of a class he had given the deacons just months before he died. His voice and presence filled the house. How he'd grown in wisdom and the ability to organize his thoughts while speaking from the heart. "I feel as though he's been here visiting this week. I feel so sharply how much I've lost," I wrote in my journal.

The young daughter of a friend died that week, and I played with my guitar group at her funeral. Once again, but from another pew, I saw the lines of cars, her family's stoic courage, felt the silence fall like a drumbeat. It cut my soul.

Our dog also died that week, the gentle retriever with

no bad habits except to stray after children. She had developed a growth on her heart. I carried her to the vet and watched her relax, the labored panting stop, as she died.

"No, no. You bury her," I said frantically and ran from the office before I cried again. The last thing I wanted was another funeral.

Back at home, I laid the baby in his seat and watched him for a moment. A moment? Or was it an hour? He looked peculiar to me. His eyes stared at me while the rest of his face melted away. Operating by instinct and habit, I carefully picked him up to change him. I could have put him in the oven like a little turkey and not have known it.

An aura of unreality had crept over my mind. My senses weren't working properly: time passed strangely, and I felt lightheaded, as though underwater. If someone had come to the door, I would have made an effort to speak coherently, but I'm not sure that I could have.

A rational part of me was terrified. Was I going crazy? What would happen to the kids if I lost it? How long would this last? Would it come back? No, I had to hold on as long as I could and do my best to act normally.

Slowly the cheesecloth lifted from my brain. Vague, formless, like a mist, it came and went. After that week of death, from then on, like a sunflower, I began to turn. School brought a predictable routine and a few hours' reprieve for me. Although I still had energy for little beyond each day's demands, I began questioning, testing, sorting out my feelings. I could not yet comprehend the enormity of my circumstances. How could he be dead, this man brimming with vitality?

This was a time of leavetaking, "laying up in

lavender" as the old ones say. It was a turning from the important "firsts": first lover, best and oldest friend, husband of my youth, the one who had marked my body and my soul. Partly it was a turning from youth itself.

Some questions refused to be neatly packaged. Our relationship had ended midstream with conflicts unresolved, good-byes unsaid, and the full flowering of maturity still a future promise. Ghosts rose up to sneer: "How good was your marriage, really? What about all the hard years? Would you have lasted anyway?"

Useless, tormenting questions, they clutched with formless fingers. A youth was invested in a relationship half-done. A family begun. Tears and laughter spent. For what?

With the turning, a restlessness grew, prodding me impatiently. Memories stung, but had softer edges now, without the piercing intensity. Sadness nibbled like a mouse at the corners of my mind. I knew the Lord had a plan for me, a purpose for my life, and I wanted to know it.

Fidgeting with impatience, I cried out, "What? What now, Lord?"

Sisters in Grief

5

Facing Forever
What we have lost

Widows. Suddenly we have joined a select community, one we had never thought to enter. We are sisters of sorrow, daughters of the void. Suddenly our identity is linked to what we have lost: husband, marriage, father of our children, friend, provider. After years of bounty, suddenly we are the empty ones.

How can this be? Why is the steady current of a life that was years in the making so utterly destroyed? Why is tomorrow so hostile and insecure? We absorb the meaning of *forever* slowly as days pass like beads on a ring, until we have totted up so many that we begin to understand—he is not coming back.

Tomorrow the sun rises, and tomorrow and tomorrow. The children ring our beds with their cereal bowls.

Day by day, we go on. We laugh again; we may even love again. But it is a different life, a new love. The first is not "recovered from," not "gotten over." When our sons and daughters marry, when a certain musical refrain wafts into consciousness, when our grandchild's eyes have just that shade of blue, we will remember. And the old scar will pinch.

Some of us became adults within this relationship. Its soft tension bent our attitudes and framed our values. It influenced our choice of toothpaste and what we ate for dinner. We did not know the weight of love until its release.

This man may have been our first love, the husband of our youth. With energy and innocence we bore our children, built our homes. "He was my high-school sweetheart," said Tammi, widowed at thirty-two with four small children. Our youth is buried with our husband.

We may have married later, a deliberate choice made with greater maturity. This was to be our last love, the one we fit so well. The time was right; we had wholeheartedly embraced the future together. Our future died with this man.

We Have Lost Our Identity

Being a wife and mother defines us to ourselves and to the world. I am this child's mother; I am that man's wife. Because of those relationships we could be the teacher's aide or belong to the ladies' auxiliary. From the investment of our lives we derived a sense of purpose and direction; these roles gave meaning and satisfaction to our lives.

"A woman's identity is largely framed by her relationships and is attached to the roles associated with these relationships," writes Dr. Phyllis Silverman, whose research on widowhood was a model for the national Widow-to-Widow program. "For a woman, the role of wife is fused with her sense of self."[1]

Besides losing an important chunk of our own identity, we have also lost a tidy niche on the social totem pole. For years we moved smoothly within familiar boundaries, doing what was expected of us and knowing what to expect of our mate, other relationships, and casual daily contacts. Everyone else was comfortable with us too—"Mrs." is easy to identify.

But a "widow," especially one with toddlers and blue jeans, is a jarring misfit. We don't know how to act in this role. The friends we made through our husband's profession or hobbies will probably fade in time. Being alone, we no longer meet the basic requirements for our couples' groups, and we lose whatever status we gained from our husband's occupation.

Hannah's husband was a musician in their city's symphony orchestra. "Everyone knew I was his wife," she said. "When we went to a party or to church, everybody would come up to me and say, 'Oh, the orchestra sounded wonderful last night.'"

Hannah's dark hair is pulled carelessly into a braid. She wears no makeup. Her beauty radiates from an inner grace and large, soft eyes. As she shares her story with me, she speaks with carefully chosen words. A writer and editor of a local magazine, she knows the vagaries of words.

Hannah's husband died of cancer eighteen months ago in a distant city where he had gone for a bone marrow transplant. The family stayed with nearby relatives so that the children, then seven and nine, could visit their father daily.

Now Hannah wears both wedding bands on her right hand. Her son will be given his father's ring when he marries. Money is as tight as a new shoe, but her job with the magazine gives her the flexibility she values as a single parent. Hannah remembers wistfully the days before her husband died, when they were courted by the media and befriended by the wealthy and powerful in town.

"I've always thought of myself as someone who doesn't really care too much about status," she said. "But I'm finding it's a hard thing to lose."

We Have Lost the Father of Our Children

With the death of our husband, we have lost the only person in the world who shared our instinctive, biological attachment to our children. That natural pride and animal protectiveness may be approximated but will never be replaced. We may have disagreed about their upbringing, but at least someone else knew our children as well and cared as much. Without ballast and soundingboard we swing erratically in our parenting before we find a new sense of balance.

Trudy's children were two and five when her husband died of a brain aneurysm. She remembers the numbness and sense of unreality that enmeshed her. A schoolteacher for many years, she went back to work functioning for a while "just like a robot." Work was the only part of life that went on almost normally and allowed her to feel competent.

Although Trudy worked with children by profession, her training was no advantage in dealing with her own. Her lively voice and quick humor contradict the almost obsessive concern she felt for her children's welfare. "I was so worried they would never recover from such a traumatic experience," she said. "I was willing to do anything to help them adjust to it.

"When Nathan rode his bike around the block I was on the curb with a stopwatch wondering why it took so long. There was no one to say, 'Relax, it's okay. He'll get around the block.'"

We Have Lost Our Marriage

Every marriage has its own personality, a sum of parts that interact uniquely. We worked, played, and communicated in distinctive ways. Some marriages were more autonomous, with separate friends, different careers, unique roles, and independent emotional lives. Perhaps our husband took care of the car and the yard while we managed the house and children. Perhaps he was the strong, silent type and we shared our feelings elsewhere; perhaps he was more sensitive and we learned to cater to his moods.

Some relationships emphasized sharing and communication and were more emotionally interdependent. Jobs and roles blended more, and husband and wife relied on each other for companionship and support.

Some relationships were ambivalent. They had an

explosive quality and a stronger love/hate polarity. These marriages were difficult to feel secure within and to resolve when they ended. Generally, the more consuming the relationship and the greater the ambivalence or dependency, the more harrowing will be the adjustment to a single life. If our husbands "took care" of everything, we must now learn new skills very quickly.

Reba was forty-one when her husband died suddenly. She had three children nearing young adulthood and two preschool boys. Her anguished cry as the ambulance pulled away with her husband's body was "God, you've given me these beautiful children. Why are you taking their daddy? You've taken my provider, my comforter. What am I going to do?"

She felt God answer her: "I'll be your provider. I'll be your comforter. I'll take care of you."

"My husband was dead," said Reba, "but God was with me in such a glorious way."

But there was no shining path through the difficulties. Reba was completely independent for the first time in her life. "A very submissive wife," she now struggled to make her own decisions and rear her children alone. During the years of their marriage, her husband had handled everything. "I had gone from reporting to my father to reporting to a husband," she told me. "I was totally dependent on him to make the decisions. He approved everything. Being widowed was a tremendous change for me."

Reba took classes on decision making and self-esteem. She studied and struggled. Sometimes she avoided her troubles; sometimes she made mistakes. But she persevered and took each step more confidently. "I learned that you don't need anyone to tell you what to do," she said. "You can find your own solutions."

Whatever the quality and character of our marriage, in the early months of widowhood we cast it in a rosy glow; we remember only the ideal parts of our relationship.

But slowly, like yeast fermenting, the flaws bubble to the surface. This was an "off-time" loss—old people die, not young men in their prime. Our relationship also ended in its prime: half-formed, with major tasks uncompleted; essential questions unanswered. We weigh and measure with guilt and anger at our elbow. Our life's investment was flawed; unfinished business is hard to bury. If our relationship was especially difficult, we may mourn a loss of hope in marriage altogether.

Perspective comes only with distance. In time we treasure the good, accommodate the bad, and make peace with the ambivalence that every relationship holds. In time we shed our empty roles and identity of loss and begin to welcome someone new.

6

Last Days
The nature of his death

Stan worked in data processing, but his real love was building things. He finally indulged that passion when he began construction on his family's new home in the country. He continued that loving labor for two and a half years after he was diagnosed with leukemia.

"He set goals and completed them," said his wife, Debby. "He was amazing that way."

Stan died far from his new home, in a hospital where he had gone for a bone marrow transplant. Debby traveled with him, shuttling between motels and the hospital for six weeks. Their children, ages six and nine, came with their grandparents to visit their father. They saw him once. He was so disfigured they didn't want to go back.

Recalling that time, Debby said, "It was almost more than I could bear, to watch that process and know that there was nothing I could do. Before he died, he went into a coma from so much pain. I have a fear of hospitals now. I know I have to get over it someday, but it's still real fresh with me."

Stan died three years ago. Debby has remarried and shares her country house with her new husband, who also lost a spouse to cancer. But the anger and horror of Stan's death still leak into her voice when the scar is scratched.

When our husband was alive we were intimately involved in the course and quality of our marriage. But we had no say in its ending. Yet how our husband died—suddenly, violently, or after a lingering illness—affects us profoundly, creating vivid memories and the emotional baggage we carry into widowhood.

Studies suggest that an expected death allows time to prepare, to mourn, to say good-bye. Yet every woman I spoke with, no matter how bleak the prognosis, expected her husband to live. "There were twelve patients in this ward," said Debby. "It was very specialized, with air filters and stuff. Every few days I would see people die, but I knew Stan wouldn't die. Right up till maybe three days before, I still thought he would get through it." Such is the unquenchable spirit of humanity; such are the adaptations we make to live in the face of death.

Diane's husband had malignant melanoma for seven of the ten years of their marriage. His disease haunted them, becoming an unwelcome partner to their lives. She has no children. After his death, she said, "I am really alone. There's no part of him left. It's almost as though he never existed."

During the eighteen months that Hannah's husband grappled with his cancer, they "let everything else just drop away," to focus on their relationship, on their family, and on managing the disease. They grew to know each other so intimately that they began to finish each other's sentences and answer questions before they were asked. "We were fighting the disease together, and we developed a relationship as close and symbiotic as people who have been married thirty or forty years," said Hannah. "We became so intertwined that eventually we were like one limb."

At first her husband's death was a release from the constant strain of illness. But gradually she was flooded with the magnitude of her loss. His death was a profound amputation.

Flashbacks of the circumstances surounding our husband's death are breathtaking and disturbing in their force and detail. If we witnessed the death, we relive it repeatedly. Instead of remembering the handsome, vital man we married, our most vivid memories may be of the crises in the hospital or of a spouse bloated or emaciated from illness.

Sudden death is quick, clean, incisive. A single, neat cut. There is no gradual assuming of roles, no forgiveness after last night's fight, no good-bye. Studies indicate that sudden deaths cause more initial numbness and greater emotional disturbance throughout the first year of bereavement. The widowed are more likely to sense the presence of the dead person and to treasure reminders of him.

When Pam's husband died in an airplane crash in Europe, she never saw his body, and it was some time before she even had his remains to put in the ground. She knows he is dead, but a tiny doubt gnaws in a closet of her mind. Maybe there was some mistake, maybe . . .

Violent death adds layers of fear, anger, and legal complication. Laura's husband was shot and another man paralyzed by a mentally unstable fellow worker who walked into the office one day and opened fire. Even before this tragedy, the employee had shown obvious signs of emotional problems but had kept her job because the union had prevented her from being fired.

Laura experiences the trauma indirectly through the employees in her husband's department. Some of them don't want to be reminded of the tragedy by even seeing her. It makes them cry.

She is angry at a system that permitted such violence and a God who failed to protect her husband. As a new trial nears for his murderer, Laura is torn between her desire to lay aside the horror or to sit in the courtroom with her two sons as silent witnesses "so they'll remember he had a wife and children."

The widow of a suicide is doubly stigmatized. Suicide is a virulent social taboo. Other people, even other bereaved, visibly recoil from the survivor of that death. Blame is often implied by others and arises powerfully from within. Survivors learn to hide the dark truth that marks them, increasing their isolation and their anguish.

"Usually, you cannot tell who [the survivors] are because, like me, they have learned not to let their emotions show," writes the widow of a suicide. "They have learned not to cry in public. They have learned that people all too often react to them with shock, condemnation, revulsion, or pity."[1]

Sometimes a husband's passing has an almost bitter-sweet beauty, like Reba's story of her husband's death.

Leon had been active in sports all his life. He played semi-pro football and at forty-three was a coach and an avid fisherman.

He was competing in a bass tournament when he broke his foot, thought nothing of it, and continued fishing. A cast was put on later, and he went back to work the next day "'cause he was that kind of guy."

It was a Sunday morning in Texas. Leon's cast would come off tomorrow. The homey Sunday routine was under way—Reba put the coffee on, Leon hobbled out for the paper.

Suddenly he appeared at the bathroom door where Reba was dressing for church. "He came in and caressed me and kissed me so tenderly. Then he held me away from him and just looked at me."

Reba was startled. Her man was a big, strong guy, not much given to affection. Over the years she had come to understand that a peck on the cheek meant "I love you." This was so unusual that she looked up at him in amazement.

"His eyes were just beautiful. I was overwhelmed and could not look away from them. He was looking at me with such love. They were like the eyes of Jesus."

Confused, she looked down. The moment her gaze lowered, Leon fell to the floor. By the time the paramedics arrived, he had been dead eight minutes from a stroke caused by a blood clot in his broken foot.

Through the hard times, Reba would remember her husband's eyes, the eyes of Jesus, which are real and vivid to her today, almost a decade later.

7

Light Through the Curtain
The pitfalls and progress of grief

How *long does grief last?*
All of it, the grinding hardness of it. This pain we have never known that relentlessly consumes us. This uncertain path that goes on and on, its ending out of sight. Sometimes we don't recognize ourselves in the anger, the confusion, and the sorrow.

How long will I be in torment?

Early research indicated that normal grieving could be resolved in a few weeks. A few weeks! As studies began to include more people over longer periods of time, a more realistic picture emerged—at some level this work of grief will last a lifetime.

How long?

Not forever, but for a while. The burning intensity of

hurt fades in a few months. The outbursts of tears slowly evaporate. Sometimes memory washes over us with breathless longing, but increasingly our former life becomes a lovely time we once lived that we will remember fondly.

Sometimes grief is resolved quickly, but more often it requires several years to absorb the trauma, adjust to the changes, and rebuild an identity and a new life suited to it. The ascent is so steep because so much change is demanded on so many levels.

"Normal" Grief

"Normal" grief can mean almost anything. Behavior once considered bizarre or pathological is now accepted as part of the process. Early theories of an intense but structured and limited period of grieving have given way to a much broader range of responses and duration.

Just as the content of our lives and the character of our relationships are unique, so is the course of our grieving. Many models have been concocted to accommodate the broad patterns of grief. While most grief models have three or four stages, some put us through a dozen at a spritely pace.

Models are convenient for psychologists to bring some order to a chaotic process and to help determine when the course has gone awry. But the model becomes a noose when it is used to label our experience or when we define our own progress against it—when we are dismissed as "just in anger" or wonder why we seem to have skipped depression.

Grief is not a lock-step progression of stages. Rather, it is a dynamic process with common features. Grief is a messy business, an eruption of the most intense bits of psyche that we keep tightly tamped down in more serene times. Unhealed ills and ungrieved losses may bubble to the surface of this cauldron, a painful brew that can take many years to work through. Childhood hurts and maladaptive ways of handling crises further impede the healing process.

There is no worn path or tidy garden steps to grieving, no timetable for being done. Some bereaved people continue to feel their loss is unresolved even decades later. At first the goal is simply to survive, to make it through one more day.

The nature of our grieving, its intensity and duration, where the process falters, and how we recover are all affected by the baggage we carry into grief. Experts have identified certain risk factors that can complicate and intensify the process: the quality of the support systems we have; how our husbands died—suddenly, violently, or after a long illness; our own personality and past experience; and other stresses in our lives, such as pregnancy or financial problems.

The way all these things juxtapose either helps our healing or hinders it and makes the grieving process unique to each of us. We weave our mourning veil of common threads: shock, confusion, anger, sadness, depression. Sometimes the scarlet of anger predominates, or black depression, or foggy hues of fear and sadness. We weave our grief of common colors, but the veil is ours, its hue and pattern unique.

Common Threads of Grief

"What do you mean you lost him in the CAT scan?" Trudy demanded. "How could you lose him? You put him in, you take him out. I don't understand." An absurd image comes to mind: an anxious wife bobs among the tubes and charts, searching for a husband who has been misplaced like a hat pin.

Another young woman, when told her husband was in full cardiac arrest, asked, "Is it life-threatening?"

"But I don't even like geraniums," Marge said repeatedly after her husband's death in a car accident. Widows had geraniums and neat Cape Cod bungalows with white picket fences. How could she be a widow without becoming reconciled to the trappings of widowhood?

If any reaction to death is universal, it is the shock, denial, numbness which immediately engulf us. We are schizophrenic in our perception; we believe but we don't comprehend. I knew my husband was dead. I could see he was dead. I understood he wasn't coming back. But . . . what did that mean? Like most of us, I was composed and capable during the funeral, but months later the unreality of it all still washed over me. He *couldn't* be dead.

"Right after he died, I really wondered if I did love him, because I didn't fall apart," said Laura, widowed at forty with two young sons. "I hardly cried until after the funeral. I kept thinking, *Boy, I must not have loved him.*"

In the months following our husband's death, we can't concentrate. We misplace everything. We go on spending sprees to make ourselves feel better. We try to keep everything as it was "before"—and drive ourselves crazy. Or we do only what is necessary, barely making it through each day. Or we let everything go and keep on running. "I think I overdid it," said Pam, exhausted after an extended European trip with her three young sons.

We long to be comforted, to be parented, to have someone take care of us, even as we resist such childlike dependency. We want to be surrounded with reminders of our husband, and we long for the security of our former lives. Sometimes we feel just fine and, maybe with a twinge of guilt, want to avoid thinking of painful things. Only in hindsight do we recognize our clouded judgment and disoriented actions.

Anger is endemic to young widows. Life has thrown us one of its nastiest knuckle sandwiches right to the chops. We have reason to be angry and we spew it everywhere, at God, our friends and family, our husbands, our doctors. "I felt my husband had jumped ship and left me with this baby," said Trudy. "I was mad at everybody." We are angry because of what we've lost, what we're left with, and how we're being treated. Rooted in fear and pain, our anger sometimes lasts a long time.

Sadness and depression are different birds of a feather. If sadness is the sparrow, depression is the black crow. Losing something valuable makes us sad. We miss what we have lost, we cry, we search for it, and we want it back. Tidal waves of sadness are probably an unavoidable part of grief and are different from depression.

A sadness without hope, depression has a clinical definition and set of symptoms. We see no light, no tomorrow that will be better. We may feel guilty, lose confidence, be immobilized. We may eat and sleep a lot less, or a lot more.

Pam describes depression as "a heavy, desperate feeling." She said, ('At times there was so much pain I didn't want to go on) I couldn't function, couldn't do anything. I'd say, 'Oh, I really ought to pay some bills or make supper.' And I'd just sit there. I wouldn't care about anything or anybody, myself included."

When Pam's husband died in a highly publicized airplane crash, she knew she was in trouble. Part of the baggage she carried into widowhood was the half-buried memory of a difficult, dysfunctional childhood. A veneer of fierce independence masked a stubborn depression. "I feel, because of my childhood, a lot of my life was spent in a low-grade depression," Pam said. "So, something like this hits and I respond characteristically."

Illness

Regaining balance and identity, untying bonds that have been created over years—the task of healing is perhaps the most difficult and dangerous we will tackle short of death itself. It taxes our bodies and our minds. In one study, almost forty percent of the bereaved feared they were going insane at one time or another. Grief was a legitimate cause of death in times past; "dying of a broken heart" has one foot in myth, one in confirmed fact.

Grief, like stress, can make us sick. It is, in fact, a most deadly stress. The death of a spouse zooms a widow to the top of the stress charts. It aggravates existing health problems and leaves us more vulnerable to illness. Studies report that younger widows actually experience greater health deterioration than older ones. We are at greater risk for mental illness and physical problems ranging from panic attacks and insomnia to cancer.[1]

Trudy's experience wasn't uncommon: "I was very sick after Ted died. I went from one illness to another. Anything within a 200-mile radius I would catch. I felt real vulnerable then."

Since this is such an acutely stressful time on all fronts, we need to take care of ourselves, develop the health habits we so zealously urge upon our children—take vitamins, eat well, play, exercise, (try to) sleep. They are just as necessary for us, too.

I'm one of the widows who regrets not taking life easier on myself and nurturing the children better in those early months of grief. Some of us run so hard and try so compulsively to maintain everything as it had been "before."

Drug and Alcohol Use

Studies show that drug and alcohol use increase among the widowed. Men tend to drink more; women get depressed and take more pills. In a 1987 survey conducted by the National Widowed Persons Service (WPS), over one-third of the respondents had been prescribed medication, usually tranquilizers, for grief-related problems.

Those who study bereavement are consistently vocal in their opposition to the use of drugs and alcohol. Grief, like adolescence, is a difficult growth passage. Using substances numbs the pain but retards the process and carries the continual risk of addiction.

In an open letter to bereaved parents, Elisabeth

Kubler-Ross writes, "I'm sharing this also with you in the hope that you *never* allow anybody to give you Valium at the time of such a crisis, as it will cheat you out of the chance to experience *all* your feelings, cry out all your pain, shed all your tears, so that you can live again, not only for your own sake, but for the sake of your family and all others whose lives you can touch!"[2]

Widows who have used drugs have a mixed response. Many felt that using drugs or alcohol was not helpful. They worried about their changed patterns of consumption and eventually had to feel bad for a while anyway.

"Sometimes I would drink and that would ease the pain," said Pam. "It didn't make me feel better; it just dulled my feelings."

While grief experts may be adamantly opposed to sedatives, our doctors see us when we can't eat, can't sleep, can't concentrate, and are generally miserable. Doctors may themselves be uncomfortable with death and with the intensity of our feelings. Reaching for the prescription tablet may seem an appropriate treatment.

Over one-third of the respondents to the WPS survey considered their doctors inadequately informed about the grief process. But two-thirds of those prescribed medication felt that it had been helpful.

Using medications prescribed to help us sleep or get through the day may be necessary during the early nightmare. We do whatever we can to make it. But substance abuse has been identified as a closet problem among the bereaved. We who must absorb so much and make so many changes are vulnerable to dependencies.

Suicidal Feelings

Substances help us avoid our grief temporarily. At some point for most of us, the ultimate avoidance lurks in the corners of our minds and sometimes leers boldly from center stage. We've lost so much and feel so bad. Why go on? It would be so easy to die.

Sometimes we decide to live because of our children. "I remember sitting on the basement floor and wishing I could die, yet not really being serious because I didn't want the boys to lose their mom," said Laura. "I often felt if I didn't have the boys to live for, I don't know how I would have survived that first year."

Sometimes our children aren't enough or they are so difficult as to be an added burden. We delude ourselves into thinking that everyone would be better off without us. "It got to the point I didn't care about my kids," one widow recalls. "I said, 'They'll manage. If I die they'll live in a family and have a mother and a father. God will take care of them.' I would think of different ways I could kill myself."

During the first months of constant pain and adjustment, death sometimes seems a welcome alternative. But the pain subsides. Life is possible again, then hopeful, maybe even exciting. Grieving comes and goes in waves of lessening intensity. The same emotions spiral round, but with diminished force.

If you think frequently of killing yourself or know how you will do it, you need to tell someone you trust. You need to be with someone who cares about you, and you need to look for ongoing help.

As one widow's therapist said as they discussed her

contemplated suicide, "Your children would never recover from your death." Neither would your friends and relatives. Neither would the world.

Finding a Listening Ear

Finding a therapist when we can barely get through the day may seem like an enormous effort—and it is. Talk with people you know: the funeral home director, other widows, the family doctor. Institutions that regularly rub shoulders with death are often most aware of local resources. Check with hospices, hospital social workers or chaplains, and leaders of grief support groups.

Get names of individuals, not groups of therapists. Schedule consultations with a few and have your questions ready. It's important to find someone whose personality and approach feels comfortable to you. Absorb the atmosphere of the office and ask about the therapist's background, experience, fee, and therapeutic approach.

A neutral, caring ear is a great release. As I dropped one child or another off for counseling appointments, I caught myself taking some of that time for my own unloading. It felt great to talk, and I knew I wouldn't see that face in the grocery store the next day.

Sensing His Presence

Once considered a bizarre and pathological aberration, experts now concede what the bereaved have long known: most of us will see or sense, hear or feel the presence of our spouse in the months and even years following his death.

This spontaneous occurrence is reassuring and familiar, not frightening. Sometimes we see our husbands in a favorite place; sometimes we simply sense that he is near or feel his touch. Whether this happens because we desire it so badly or as an afterglow of the life and love we shared, the experience is baffling, common, and comforting.

Marie had just cleaned out her nightstand. A little later, looking for a piece of paper, she opened the drawer and found a note lying on top in her husband's script: "Marie, I love you so very much."

"It always bugged me," she said. "It made me feel good but I've always wondered how it got there."

Shortly after her husband's death, Debby dreamed with startling clarity that he had called her on the phone, reassuring her that he was in the best possible place and not to worry about him. "I believed it was him and it has given me comfort. I feel better about death and dying," she said.

A widower described a poignant enounter with his wife nine months after she had died. He had been going through a particularly hard time and stopped one morning at her grave, telling her how hard life was for him and how much he missed her.

That morning at work, she suddenly appeared to him, with "her hair down, just the way I liked it." She assured him that she was well, "at home," and happy. His depression lifted; he felt peaceful and encouraged.

This phenomenon is more likely to occur when the death was sudden or the marriage of long duration. But it isn't moved by our desiring, seeming tuned to other laws and seasons. Intimate as Hannah's marriage had become during the months of her husband's illness, much as she wanted, and expected, to sense his return, it didn't happen. "I've gone to bed sometimes and said, 'Tonight, okay? You can come tonight.'" But he doesn't, and by day she laughs and says, "Jim won't come. The house is too messy."

Flying Solo

How long will it take to heal? No one knows. We are a complicated web of attachments, relationships, personal strengths, and past experience that constellate to our benefit or misfortune.

The best advice I found was in a children's book: don't try to make yourself feel better or worse. Grief increases—like the pain of childbirth—when we clutch against it. I tried to let feelings flow, neither avoiding pain nor feeling guilty for feeling good.

Intense crisis tests us at every level but also creates possibilities we might never have expected. We may someday pursue interests that never fit before, learn new skills, develop an identity and relationships based on many roles, not just "wife."

Learning to fly solo takes time. Such major life alterations as new career goals, a satisfying social niche, and skill with a rachet wrench come gradually with effort and practice. The first flights are exhilarating, but until new muscles and nerves are strong and developed, as Hannah says, "I don't have to conquer this today."

Many women emphasized the importance of finding

other young widows. We are awake at 2:00 A.M. and are free evenings and weekends. We know that spending sprees are normal, offer an empathetic ear for troubles with the kids, and can commiserate about the quirks of being such a social misfit.

One widow found it healing to surround herself with beauty—nature, music, art. She accepted help when it was offered and leaned on the support systems available to her. Such good advice is difficult for the stiff-necked like myself to follow. Life might have been easier for me had I graciously accepted the hands outstretched to me.

Life trickles back, bubbling unquenched through tiny crevices. My little ones chattered and played at the foot of their father's coffin. I was grateful for that vitality.

One day you smile reflexively or crack a joke without even thinking about it. One morning you notice light creeping into the window much earlier than before. Spring has come, slowly, like all growth.

8

Fellowship of Love
Suffering unites

I almost envy you." The young woman sat across from me at the dining room table several weeks after Richard's death. Usually composed and self-assured, she faltered as she spoke, wondering if I would understand.

Her life was enviable, with an apple-pie wholesomeness. With two young boys and an involved doctor-husband, she had no skeletons peering from her closets. Hers were the normal struggles of a wife and mother trying to live and raise her children within Christian values. Who could want a better life?

But I did understand. Days pass in effortless monotony and we forget to treasure them. We miss the sparkling curiosity in our children's eyes. We grumble at the weeds but neglect the morning glories bobbing near the fence post.

Faith is a habit with frayed sleeves, a comfortable garment we shrug on to work in the garden. Where is our first love? How can we recapture the early zeal? And more worrisome, how would our everyday faith fare under uncommon crisis? We hunger to be tested. With a twinge of anxiety we proclaim with Peter, "Lord, at your side I am prepared to face imprisonment and death itself."

But by evening Peter had sworn to the servant girl that he knew nothing of his Lord. Would we do any better?

From the valley of my testing I looked dumbly at this woman. What could I say to her? Go home and see your treasures with new eyes? Love your husband and children as though this is the last day you will have them—because it may be?

Perhaps suffering is not necessary for holiness, although the holy ones of God seemed to endure much. Humility and compassion can be cultivated without trials. And suffering creates broken, angry people as well as soft, loving ones. Knowing the pain of loss and its reverberations through the years, I would not ask for trials.

Yet suffering is a mystery and a privilege that I only dimly understand. All humanity suffers; most people endure pain and loss at some time in their lives. Some stories are so extreme, we wonder how the victims can survive. Sometimes I'm sure they don't.

Pain of any sort has the power to crush or humble, to warp or ennoble. Death and growth lie within its veils. The stark and utter silence of God hanging in naked vulnerability from a cross is part of that mystery. "Look," it says, "this is important, necessary. Ponder the depths of this paradox."

"You have to remove your shoes before someone in pain," a friend once said. "It is something sacred." In the crucible of suffering, the fire of divinity refines the scraps of our humanity. Suffering is indeed a sacred process.

The crucible births a capacity for compassion, and tolerance for another's pain. Instead of feeling discomfort and drawing back, instead of averting our eyes and mumbling our sympathy, we who suffer well have learned the value of shared tears and a loving touch.

I have not been sainted by suffering. If anything I am more aware of my own discomfort, clumsiness, and avoidance. But a seed has been planted. While Richard was alive I learned of suffering through him, watching as he grew in gentle wisdom. Now the lessons are intimately mine, to touch what is most profoundly human and learn from it.

In my own trouble I felt the fellowship of the valley. Through the stripping and destroying of everything secure, I am linked to suffering humankind everywhere and throughout time. I have entered an ocean of human lamentation.

In his book *Healing into Life and Death*, Stephen Levine described the unifying power of suffering. He writes of Hazel, an angry, grasping person throughout her life who came to the hospital to die, in great pain and abandoned even by her children.

> For six weeks her isolation and pain increased until one night something changed. She came to a point where she could no longer stand the suffering in

her back and legs, or the pain of her unlived life. At four A.M., feeling like jumping out of her skin, she began to review her life amidst the pulsations of her pain. . . .

Feeling death approach, she remembered herself as a youngster, open and hungry for the world. She saw how she had closed down over the years. With a deep sigh she let the helplessness wash over her and, exhausted, unable to fight another moment, she surrendered, she let go and "died into her life," into the moment. Letting go into the pain in her spine and legs, she began to sense, quite beyond reason, that she was somehow not alone in her suffering. She felt what she later called "the ten thousand in pain." She began to experience all the other beings who at that very moment were lying in that same bed of agony. At first there arose the experience of herself as a brown-skinned woman, breasts slack from malnutrition, lying on her side, a starving child suckling at her empty breast, spine and legs twisted in pain, the musculature contracted from starvation and disease. For an instant, she became this Ethiopian woman with this same pain in the back and legs and hips, lying on her side, dying in the mud. Then there arose the experience of an Eskimo woman lying on her side dying during childbirth, tremendous pain in her back, hips, and legs and dying the same death. Then her experience became that of the body of a woman in a twisted car wreckage, her back and legs broken, slowly dying alone by the side of a deserted road.[1]

At this eleventh hour Hazel's life opened to compassion. She begged forgiveness of her children, expressed concern about those dying around her, cared for her caretakers. "Her room became a place of healing, of finished business, of universal care." She died a few weeks later, gazing at a picture of Jesus, the Good Shepherd.

In reaching the edges of human experience, in the crucible of pain, we can enlarge our hearts to greater compassion. We can learn to "suffer with," so that our suffering becomes a privilege.

However, the bitterness of loss will never transform into compassion without a spirit of gratitude. In any circumstance we have much to be grateful for. "I became really grateful that my husband hadn't died before we were married or before we'd had children," said Trudy. "At least we had accomplished certain things. Gratitude took my anger away."

Even as I held the infant who would never know his father, I felt lucky to have five healthy children, lucky for the financial stability to be home with them, lucky for my friends and family who cared for me. It really could have been so much worse.

Gratitude is a lubricant in the work of healing, smoothing the grinding gears of pain. We feel gratitude most when we are loved, when those around us extend their hands. Then the circle is complete. Those who are strong enter into the valley of suffering, and those who suffer are helped toward wholeness.

But a hand must be extended, and it must be grasped. Suffering can bear no fruit if the one who suffers remains in the bitterness of isolation. If no one reaches out, or the sufferer is unwilling or unable to grasp the helping hand, brokenness remains.

Yes, friends and family can be hurtful and insensitive. Acquaintances will be uncomfortable and unable to see

I had Likened it to the Scarlet Letter!

beyond the black W imprinted on our foreheads. Some will avoid us, and others will force their charity upon us.

But those silent acts of caring we do receive shine like a full moon on a black night, throwing silver on our path. They draw us into warmth when we feel so awkward and alone.

Although she often feels "dumped" by friends, Pam's church sent dinner over once a week for a year. "I was very grateful for that. It was a simple act that made a difference to me," she said.

Sometimes God sends an angel. Laura was walking to the car in an icy parking lot with another couple. "I was slipping and sliding on the ice and she was snug and secure on her husband's arm," Laura recalled. Before resentment had too firm a grip, a man's voice said in her ear, "Let me help you," and a sure arm guided her to the car. "I felt it was a kiss on the cheek from God," Laura said.

I am grateful beyond words for the arms that upheld me. Without them my life and the lives of my children would be impoverished, financially and emotionally.

The donations that poured in allowed me "breathing room." For the first time in years I could afford small luxuries that made my life easier or more beautiful. I could ease up a bit on my stinginess. I could take the kids out to dinner for good report cards, get repairs done on the house, buy a shampoo a cut above the generic brand.

But kindness with a human face meant the most. I was constantly overwhelmed with gratitude for the loving acts of the people around me. Week after scorching week that first summer, Jim rattled our decrepit mower over our half acre, patching the machine each time with twine and chewing gum. He asked for nothing, not lunch or gratitude, and was with difficulty coaxed in for a chat and iced tea.

Bob stopped by now and then after work, doing the odd jobs that he noticed needed doing. Larry gave me a guided tour of a car's innards. Mike, barely out of his teens, spent an afternoon taming an overgrowth of shrubbery. Doug and Mary took me out to the first real dress-up restaurant I'd been to in years. Light-headed from good food and stimulating company, I floated home braced for the yoke again.

Three different crews organized painting parties that left the house sparkling inside and out. For months women I hardly knew brought special meals, lovingly prepared. Jean and Dave, the greatest neighbors ever, stood staunchly by for emergency baby-sitting and help with the mechanical breakdowns that came as sure as sunrise.

This outpouring of care was invaluable. When everything in my life, including my emotions, teetered on the brink of chaos, I could view a manicured lawn and a clean home in good repair. At least they were under control instead of mirroring my inner state. And the gratitude that overwhelmed me kept my spirit soft. How dare I freeze into bitterness when such warmth surrounded me?

Certainly, the lonely days stacked themselves like dominos; things broke and no one came to fix them; insensitive comments and even rebuffs happened occasionally. But the consistent remembrances and small charities slowly prodded me toward gratitude and growth.

And so I have a debt to pay. I owe my healing to these people, and I am bound to complete the circle. As hands reached out to me, now I must reach out. I am indentured; my task is to continue growing in sensitivity and compassion. The wheat is golden in the fields, and I must learn to use the scythe.

9

Why?
Faith sustains

What do you believe about the world? Do you believe that everything happens for a reason? That if you are a good person, if you pray and work hard, good things will come to you? Do you believe that God answers prayer? That life is fair?

Is it important to you to be in control? Who is in control?

We all have basic assumptions about how life works. Perhaps we were taught them and our experience has reinforced them. Perhaps we developed them through our own thought and observation. We may never have clearly articulated some of these assumptions, yet they influence our attitudes and responses to life situations.

Crisis leans heavily on our assumptions about life.

Some of our ideas may shatter, others are strained or readjusted, and others stand firm. With the loss of our husband, what we thought was true and dependable—our marriage, our beliefs about death and God, the safety of our world and health of our bodies—has begun to heave and quake. What can we count on?

While our worldview is in the process of reformation, life may seem fearful, even hostile. But once our worldview is examined, winnowed, and tempered, we can emerge with stronger beliefs and a firmer identity.

Hannah almost died of rheumatic fever as a child. She spent long hours alone in bed, ill and knowing something was seriously wrong. She also lived in Guatemala for three years, absorbing the extreme poverty and the brutality of civil war. These childhood experiences shaped her assumptions. She learned that life can be precarious; it owes us nothing. When her husband died, she said, "I wasn't raised with the expectation that life would be perfect and everybody deserves to live until they're seventy-five. I think that's one of the reasons I don't feel a great deal of anger about Jim's death."

In Guatemala when someone says, "See you tomorrow," the response is, "God willing." Guatemalans make no assumptions about tomorrow. Even its dawning is grace. Because we are a privileged people living in a wealthy land, we can expect that tomorrow will come for us, that we will eat and have a place to sleep. When tomorrow doesn't come as we expect, our assumptions about the world undergo major structural damage.

Crisis, according to the proverb, is "opportunity riding on dangerous winds." Crisis alters our expectations and changes the way we experience life. We learn to take less for granted and to accept what we have as a gift. Perhaps through crisis we learn to say, "God willing."

Just before her husband's death, Reba endured a severe financial crisis. Through the daily, humiliating struggle to pay the bills she learned that God could be trusted, sometimes in startling ways. "Through those times, God was teaching me how to pray about financial things," she said. "I really grew from that experience. I learned to pray specifically for each thing I needed."

Although she had particularly intense fears about money after her husband's death, Reba also found that the lessons of her first crisis held up during the second. God could be counted on to provide for her. As she trusted his providence, it came.

Yet faith is not always strengthened, prayers fulfilled, or questions answered through crisis. Suffering is not always redemptive. Crisis brings us to a fork in the road; it forces us to choose. Many people watch loved ones die, praying desperately for a miracle. When the miracle does not come, they taste only bitterness and can see no meaning, no reason for this death.

"They say God doesn't make mistakes, but maybe he did this time," said Marge. "I remember looking very hard for some good that might come of this tragedy."

We assume that events happen for reasons we can understand. When we can't find those reasons, we may gently relinquish what we do not understand. Marge decided, "I may know the answer someday, but it doesn't happen to be today." Trudy prayed for her husband's recovery from a brain aneurysm. Shortly before his death, she found peace in the Lord's Prayer: "Thy will be done."

Or we may clutch our shattered assumptions resentfully. Debby prayed intensely while her husband was dying of cancer. Although she is still somewhat active in her church, her husband's agonizing death left her feeling betrayed. "I don't know what good my prayers did," she said. "I haven't been able to make sense of the whole thing."

The way we make sense of our loss, how or if we apportion blame, and what forces, if any, we believe are in control color our experience of death.

In one study a group of researchers predicted that those for whom religion provided an important system of beliefs and attitudes would more quickly find meaning in a significant loss. But they found no correlation. While "religious" people did adjust better following a tragedy, they didn't find meaning in it. They had no explanation, no reasons, no answer to the question "why."[1]

Faith frees us from the need to find meaning in loss. The answer to our insistent "Why?" is "Just because"—as we so often tell our children. We trust because love guides us.

Faith also delivers us from the temptation to believe that events are random and inchoate, that life is meaningless. Faith doesn't provide answers; it stands silently—pointing. It whispers rather than shouts, draws instead of pushing. "Faith is being sure of what we hope for and certain of what we do not see" (Hebrews 11:1).

Although our questions may not be answered and our anger may continue to smolder, most of us who had faith before our loss will return to it afterwards. "We don't lose our faith," said Mary Anthony, a WPS group leader. "We just get mad at God."

We may question some of the beliefs that we have

lived with quite comfortably for many years. The face of God may even change for us. After Richard's death, I experienced the fatherhood of God for the first time. I felt his protective, nurturing strength. I saw God as larger, more universal and omnipotent, yet also as tenderly brooding over my trouble.

"God lets you do what you need to do," said Pam, who could not open her Bible or pray for months. "He doesn't punish or reject you for it. If the house is built on rock, the rains come, the tornado blows through, the shutters come off, but the house is still standing."

Faith, like grief, is as individual as our fingerprint. Some people have an immediate and lasting sense of God's presence; others reject God or never sense him at all. Faith for some is a sustaining wall; others avoid it until the hurt subsides and they can reintegrate their faith into their lives. Yet the repeated promise of the Bible resounds with comfort: "Here I am! I stand at the door and knock. If anyone hears my voice and opens the door, I will come in and eat with him, and he with me" (Revelation 3:20).

The unique mystery of Christianity is just that: the Omnipotent is among us; he has gone before us on the same path. The finger of faith points to Jesus, to an infinite God who shut himself within our infinitesimal frailty. What kind of God is this? What kind of love?

This is a God who knows the creature well. A God who knows the desert and has nurtured the mystery of its silent blossoming.

> The Spirit is poured upon us from on high
> and the desert becomes a fertile field,
> and the fertile field seems like a forest.

> *Justice will dwell in the desert*
> *and righteousness live in the fertile field.*
> *The fruit of righteousness will be peace;*
> *the effect of righteousness will be*
> *quietness and confidence forever.*
> *(Isaiah 32:15–17)*

Children of Grief

10

Death and the Children
Healing the little ones

The autumn routine had already begun. *Too soon*, thought Tammi as she packed her son's lunchbox and laid out his clothes. Tomorrow her eldest child would begin first grade.

Petite with sandy hair and a coil of energy under a sheen of calm, Tammi was on maternity leave from her old nursing job. The new baby was three months old; two preschool children were three and four. The cogs of a sweetly familiar life turned smoothly as she cuddled the baby and caught the last, nostalgic scent of summer.

In the morning, Tammi's husband, Jack, dropped their son off at school and went to work at the construction company he owned with his brother. They discussed the day's work, and Jack volunteered to unload concrete at a job site. Hours later his brother found Jack, who had been killed by a chunk of concrete that had fallen from the truck.

When Tammi kissed her husband good-bye at the funeral home, she promised, "I'll do my best, Jack, to raise these kids."

Suddenly Single Parents

Children are the greatest complication of young widowhood. Being a good parent is tough enough even with two to share the job. Now we are alone, rearing a family traumatized by major loss. Frozen in our own desolation, we brood over our wounded little ones. We fear for the scars they will carry; we shrink from their pain, which mirrors and magnifies our own and which we feel helpless to relieve.

We just want our children to be all right but are unsure where to turn if they are not. Our confidence as parents is shaky and our emotional stamina depleted. We don't know what to expect or how to judge our children's behavior. What is normal grief and what are the normal quirks of growing up? Where is that amorphous line whose crossing means our child needs help? Afraid and over-whelmed, we often see our children's behavior selectively and are confused by what we see.

Dr. Phyllis Silverman, who co-directed a study on childhood bereavement at Harvard Medical School, points out that the needs of children cannot wait while we mourn, yet grief hinders us from seeing and responding appropriately to our children's needs.[1]

Looking back, I recognize my own clouded vision. While I feared for my children's stability, I also feared for my own. I was confused by their silence and their apparent lack of grief, yet I overlooked or misinterpreted the behavior I couldn't understand. Because I so wanted my children to be "all right," I ignored (yes, denied) the depth of their hurt and the length of time it lasted—and continues to last.

I'm sure, like most of us, I somehow communicated to my children that I didn't want to see their grief. Their pain hurt me. I know I was uncomfortable sharing my own. And they, like most children, were so attuned to my nonverbal cues that they became obediently silent.

So we are relieved when our children go out to play as usual, even when we resent such a carefree attitude. We may be puzzled by their oblique statements and questions, concerned about behavior changes, bothered by the sudden outbursts or periodic withdrawal. We may be driven crazy by their hyperactivity and aggressive play. Sadness and crying we could recognize as grief; these reactions are maddening and confusing.

Pam's oldest boy, just entering adolescence, erupted in anger after his father's death. Some weeks after the funeral he was baby-sitting for his younger brother when both disappeared. Unresponsive to his mother's frantic calls, and to the police search that followed, he finally sauntered out, hours later, unharmed and with his brother. They had been hiding in the barn. This behavior was unprecedented, uncharacteristic, and is still unexplained.

I have since learned that children speak a more veiled language. While our children will feel and be confused by the same emotions of grief experienced by an adult, their way of communicating feelings, their grieving process, and their understanding of death depend greatly upon their stage of development and previous experience.

Infants and Young Children

A small baby can "miss" a familiar person as soon as he can keep in mind an object when it is out of sight—the stage of "object constancy," which begins at about six months. While infants can't conceive of death or the passage of time, they can and do miss an absent parent. They will also "mirror" their mother's grief, becoming upset because she is upset. At this age, any reaction to loss will be overt and clear, but beyond earliest infancy these responses become more disguised.

Children as young as two years have some concept of "dead." They have seen dead animals and insects and wondered about the creatures' immobility, whether they feel pain, and what will happen to the bodies.

But to young children, death is reversible and temporary. They surround it with fantasy and magical thinking as they do everything else in their world. After the space shuttle *Challenger* exploded, first graders would typically draw the astronauts floating safely back to earth. If their bodies were in pieces, the children thought they could be made whole. "When you are six you still believe in magic," said a young woman in one study. "I kept thinking he [her father] would be just around the corner."[2]

Several women noticed that their small children still waited for their fathers to return as they had seen him come before. Two-year-old Sally got upset when she saw her father's car. "It was easier for her when we got rid of his things," said Trudy.

Reba's little boys also waited for their dad to come home. "I would see those innocent boys waiting on the porch," she said. "He had been taken away in an ambulance, so whenever they saw one they thought their dad was coming back. That was so difficult for me."

Children under five are considered especially vulnerable to a parent's death. They may become clingy and anxious or regress to a younger developmental age—wetting the bed, wanting a bottle or blanket, not talking or walking. They may seem unaffected and go out to play as usual, or they may become hyperactive and destructive. They may be angry at the desertion of one parent and the preoccupation of the other. Some children seem bewildered and ask the same questions over and over; others quietly withdraw and appear to be coping well.

Because of their limited verbal skills, young children tend to act out memories and emotions in play. They may repeat the games and familiar activities they shared with the dead parent or play funeral or pretend to be dead. After visiting her dying father in the hospital, Hannah's daughter would bounce on her aunt's trampoline for hours composing songs about death and hospitals.

Beverly Raphael, a researcher who has observed hundreds of bereaved children, noticed that "profound themes of longing for the lost parent showed in many ways; perhaps the most poignant was reflected in the large number of parent dolls that were 'lost' during various play sessions—kidnapped and hidden away—not to be 'found,' but treasured by the children as some sort of symbolic representation of their unrequited yearning."[3]

If four-year-old Luke acted out his grief symbolically, I missed it. He would occasionally blurt to some stranger, "My dad died" or "I want a new daddy," but usually he seemed his sweet, well-adjusted self. When I spoke with him recently about his memories and feelings, he squirmed and cried a little, but doesn't remember much about that time. I sense in him a profound hurt that at age nine he still can't express and doesn't like to feel.

Children grieve in bits over time, not in the sustained, intense manner of adults. They may take years to slowly integrate and understand the significance of their loss. What a five-year-old doesn't comprehend, denies, or can't stand to feel may be pondered and mourned, when, as an adult, his first child is born or he reaches the age of his father's death.[4]

Latency: Childhood's Middle Years

By the beginning of latency, at about seven or eight years, children have a more evolved understanding of death. They know it is irreversible and inevitable but may be less sure of its causes and whether they, too, will die. Dr. Neil Kalter conducts support groups for bereaved children as part of a study at the University of Michigan. In his groups children want direct answers. "They don't want any dancing around the issues, they want the straight facts," Dr. Kalter said. "They want to talk about funerals and what they mean. Individually they may avoid issues and questions, but that's not at all true in groups."

Latency-aged children may not cry or express much feeling. They know their parent is dead but may deny the emotional impact of the loss. Boys especially may become aggressive or angry, to the detriment of their siblings or their toys. It's too dangerous to be angry at the dead parent who abandoned them, so they transfer their hostility to the surviving parent, who unfairly receives a double blast of anger. "It's hard to live with," said Dr. Kalter, "but it's not meant personally. It's there to protect against overwhelming, scary, lonely feelings."

In these middle years, children may be unclear about how things die. They become anxious about the welfare of the living parent and may be afraid to leave home or go to school. Since her husband's death from a brain aneurysm, Trudy no longer tells her children when she has a headache. It makes them too upset. Now she tells them she is taking aspirin for a stomachache.

In dealing with the trauma of the death of a parent, children still resort to the comfort of magical thinking. A woman in one study who at age thirteen had lost her mother simply imagined her away on a shopping trip to New York. Ten years later, this young woman began to integrate her loss emotionally. "It really hit me at my aunt's funeral last year when I saw my mother's tombstone. I cried like a baby."[5]

Children may also take on some of the habits, roles, mannerisms, or interests of the dead parent. This behavior is a way of comforting themselves and is often temporary. But identifying too closely with his parent can make a child afraid that he will also die like his parent.

I suspect this fear lay beneath Joe's adamant refusal to swim in Lake Michigan on our first visit there over two years after his father's drowning. In time he laid aside that anxiety and now enjoys the beautiful lake we have come to live near.

Explaining Death to Children

Children of all ages need to be told immediately, clearly, and simply what has happened to their parent. We need to explain the facts of death in a way they can understand and adapt our explanation to their age and maturity level. They need to know that their parent is not coming back and what has happened to the body. We should encourage their questions and listen for misunderstanding.

Young children believe literally what they are told. Perhaps we can all recall lingering notions from childhood when we knew absolutely that swallowing watermelon seeds made babies and that it could rain cats and dogs. Explaining a parent's death to small children is like treading a minefield of misconceptions. No one wants to believe it happened in the first place, and a child has only limited experience with death. The facts are often bewildering to a little one and may need repeating over time.

I remember the moment of choosing words to tell my children of their father's death. I didn't say that Dad had died. Half-consciously, I said "drowned," which I knew might not be clearly understood by the younger children. It was my own little denial; I didn't want to say the word.

I never thought to ask what four-year-old Luke understood. Did he know what "drowned" meant? Did he know his father wasn't coming back? I've since learned that the anxiety of not knowing or of having a distorted understanding of a parent's death is far more damaging than the pain of grief.

Three common questions about death that children may or may not express are: Did I cause this? Will it happen to me? Who will take care of me now?

I had dismissed the notion that children may feel that they caused their parent's death. I never noticed any signs of such guilt. However, Luke told me later that he had felt responsible for his father's death because he hadn't urged him to stay home. How easily I could have eased that anxiety by asking him about it!

Most important, our children need to know what will happen to them now that their father is gone. They need quick reassurance that they will be taken care of as before.

Children also need to know what happened to their father's body; they should be encouraged, but not forced, to see it. The reality of death is more difficult to accept, even for adults, when there is no body to view. I think of my friend Pam, whose husband died in an airplane crash and who, even years later, harbors a tiny doubt about his death. Children have the same need for information and reality testing, yet we often misguidedly "protect" them, and ourselves, from it.

In a 1982 study of children who had lost a parent, sixty percent of children ages two to eight didn't partici-pate in funeral services and never saw their parent's body. Researcher Beverly Raphael noted that "Since many of these deaths were the sudden and unanticipated deaths of young parents who had often left home alive and well and had subsequently 'vanished' for no reason that the child could readily understand (or was told), it was little wonder that confusion and fantasy reigned."[6] Two young children in this study hadn't been told what had happened to their parent even after two weeks.

My son, Stevie, was born two months after his father's death. I began telling him about his "Richard-daddy" when he was three. He was intensely interested and for some time afterward would spontaneously repeat the story or question me about it.

Months later, alone at the beach with his "Craig-daddy," he suddenly asked, "Did my Richard-daddy die?" Taken aback, his stepfather answered yes. "Tell me about it," prompted Steve, with the quicksilver wisdom of a very small child. Once again the story was repeated by a trusted adult. He still ponders that story and sometimes asks questions about dying and what happens to bodies and spirits.

Explaining Heaven

Religious beliefs are comforting if they have been an ongoing part of family life. But "heaven" is a tough concept for little ones. Often they think of heaven as a place like any other from which Dad will return. A child in one study thought his father was on the roof like Santa because that was the highest "up" he could imagine. Even little Stevie, years removed from the emotional impact of death, stumbled over the body-in-the-ground, spirit-with-God concept.

Every child deserves to hear what you truly believe. For all of us, heaven is hard to conceptualize, especially when we imagine our husbands there. Our soothing answers sometimes deflect our children's questions or miss the anxiety behind them ("Don't cry. Daddy is happy in heaven now."). Evaded questions or misunderstood answers leave a residue of apprehension and mistrust. Better to say "I don't know" than to tell uncertain stories.

My children have been comforted by imagining their father in heaven. They are satisfied that he is happy and feel he is still accessible to them. During church services, Esther would ask to speak to Dad, as though Jesus were handing over the phone.

However, children may harbor the same anger toward God that we feel. Dr. Kalter said, "If you talk about God's will, it may make your child pretty mad at God. But at least the child has someone to be mad at. It's much easier to be mad at God than at a dead dad."

Significance of a Parent's Death

The death of a parent is a crushing loss for a child. "There are no peaceful deaths for parents of young children. Whenever we merely say 'his parent died' we leave out the inevitable horror and tragedy that such a death entails," writes Erna Furman for a group of therapists who conducted a landmark study on childhood bereavement.[7]

Studies show that children who have had some previous exposure to death are better prepared to cope with the loss of someone close. When a child's first experience of death is the loss of a parent, his emotions are too intense and denial too strong to comprehend it. He must simultaneously absorb both the concept of death itself and its personal significance—what it means to lose someone so important to him.

With fewer coping skills and limited experience, a child may be overwhelmed by the same emotions an adult feels—fear, anger, guilt, and helplessness. Yet, unlike adults, a child is truly helpless and depends mainly on his parents to meet all his physical and emotional needs. No other relationship will be so intense, no other death so potentially damaging.

This death is an immediate, personal threat to a child who is so dependent upon so few. A child will not quickly resolve this loss. He will integrate it slowly for the rest of his life as he grows in maturity and understanding.

Surviving

We are the survivors. We live every minute not only with our own grief, but also with that of our children. And not only with grief but with the continual, physical demands of holding all our lives together, of keeping the whole show running.

We do whatever we can to survive. Tammi remembers greeting her new neighbors, only half joking, "If you hear screaming in the woods, don't worry. It's just me. Sometimes I go into the woods and scream."

She recalls the "crazy little things" that happened, such as the time all four of her children, including the baby, came down with chicken pox a month after her husband's death. And she remembers parking in front of the grocery store, bedding the kids down with quilts and toys in the back of the station wagon, and begging the cashier to come and find her if they honked. "Usually someone would have to go to the bathroom," she said.

From our need to survive springs the "conspiracy of silence" therapists often see within our families. Because the effort of regrouping as functional families is so consuming, we do not talk or share our common grief. We experience and express grief differently than our children, and, I think, some children are characteristically more private; they just don't tend to talk about their feelings. Others struggle simply to understand what has happened and how they feel about it, and some children put their feelings on the shelf until they can deal with them.

"I think my kids adjusted really well," said Debby. "My nine-year-old son verbalized a lot. My daughter [six years], didn't. Both were in a support group for bereaved children. My son didn't like it because a lot of the kids were having discipline problems. My daughter just liked being around other kids who had lost their dads."

Trudy's five-year-old son went back to school the day of the funeral. "Life just went on for him," she said. "He's real reserved and doesn't talk much about his feelings. I think that's just how he dealt with it."

Leading children through grief is unspeakably difficult, even for professionals. Erna Furman writes, "Throughout [our work with bereaved children], in our direct contacts with our patients and their families, in our private thinking and in our research discussions, we lived with the intense distress, pain, and anguish engendered by bereavement. We have come to understand that this emotional stress is an inevitable burden for all who work with bereaved children."[8]

Under the extreme pressure of our husband's death we

can't possibly do everything well. We can try to be aware of our children's needs and our own denials. We can try to express our grief openly. We can correct our course down the road if need be, and we can trust that grace will fill our lack. We can only try.

11

Families in Flux
Surviving adolescence;
forming new families

Christopher was angry. His father was dead and now he had to make room for a stepfather. For a year he had endured this intruder in the midst of his family, next to his mother. Now that they were getting married, would he have to call this stranger "Dad"?

But the change that kept him awake at night and sometimes drove him out his bedroom window to wander dark streets in agitation was his family's impending move. He would begin high school in another town; he would lose his friends, his childhood home. Everything safe and familiar was changing, and all against his will.

So Christopher stole some useless things—chewing tobacco and candy—and he was caught. His mother and stepfather spent the first evening after their honeymoon at the police station. Years later, when his anger found a voice, he asked his mother, "How could you do that to me? That time was terrible. Terrible."

Adolescence is a time of turmoil. Parents of adolescents are dragged into endless arguments with formerly sweet and docile children, unceasing worry about their activities when they are out, and nagging anxiety about the hapless world upon which these impetuous creatures will be unleashed.

Adolescence has been described as a passage similar to grief itself. Both passages begin in loss and mature in turmoil, and both shape and refine those who endure the discomfort of the process. For the adolescent, security and innocence wane before the fierce independence of adulthood. Childish ideals and fantasies wither under the harsh light of reality. Depression, fear, restlessness, and anger stalk both adolescent and mourner.

Adolescence is a time of swift change and growth. And change at this age is often fraught with stress and loss. This adult in chrysalis is wrapping up unfinished childhood business and discovering his own identity and life direction. A parent's death weighs heavily upon this process. To a teen's search for "Who am I?" is added "without my father?"

Every adolescent is exquisitely aware of the rules of the social game. Showing weakness, expressing strong emotion, being different in any unwilled way violate the ironclad code of teen conformity. That's what drove one high school girl to the basketball game a few days after her father's funeral. She *had* to go—and she must not cry.

The thrust of adolescent growth is toward independence. A parent's death sucks the teen back into childish feelings of helplessness. He doesn't want to feel helpless and he doesn't want to need his parents so much. His father's death complicates the forceful drive for independence and fuels the tendency toward aggressive acting out.

Acting Out

For adolescents, acting out is an acceptable way to be cool in front of peers while crying out for adult help and attention. Returning to school after the funeral, my son became known as "Joe Cool," the class clown, a manic and sometimes troublesome persona. He was awarded a dozen detentions that year, and I heard from every authority figure in his life, including the bus driver.

In keeping with our dominant male roles, boys tend to vent their emotions in delinquent, risk-taking behavior. They may get into fights, abuse drugs and alcohol, shoplift, and generally test the limits of authority. Surly and argumentative, they aren't much fun at home, either.

Teenage hostility and hurt invaded the early months of Anne's widowhood. Her stepson had been abandoned by his mother as a baby and now had lost his father. "He really rebelled," Anne said. "He took his anger out on me, and I did the same. We really clashed."

Reba's son was also sixteen when his father died and also went through a time of rebellious anger. "He went from being the youngest to having two little brothers to being the man of the family," said Reba. At eighteen he moved out and got married.

Both young men are now doing well. Anne eventually reconciled with her stepson; at his third wedding anniversary Reba's son said, "Mom, I know you didn't approve of my marriage, but it probably kept me out of prison."

Studies suggest that boys in early adolescence are especially vulnerable to a father's death. With his newly emerging sexuality a teenage boy is uncomfortable with emotional closeness to his mother. Dr. Kalter calls it the "porcupine defense." He said, "A boy will do everything he can to hurtfully push away those around him because he feels some sense of threat about being too close." Unconsciously, boys fear helplessness and the loss of freedom. They resist expressing or even feeling hurt and need: male models just don't permit it.

Girls have more social permission to be dependent and to express emotion. They tend to idealize their dead fathers, and some act out by seeking the comfort, reassurance, and male attention that they miss at home in sexualized relationships elsewhere.

Not all teens act out, of course. Despite the pressures many of our sons and daughters will do well. They will grieve and adjust and become the mature adults we have hoped for. And even then we worry. Marge still wonders if her grown son, a doctor, was *too* good after his father's death more than a decade ago. She worries that he repressed feelings that may surprise him later. What a relief if that were our only worry!

Most of the outrageous and maddening behavior we see in our teenagers is part of the normal and delicate phase of emerging from the cocoon. This tremendous effort continues despite the loss of their father. Life tends to sweep our children toward continued growth, maturity, and healing.

When to Find Help

Adjusting to the death of a parent is harrowing for our children, and each child responds uniquely to loss. No one, adult or child, grieves according to textbook norms, and many books on grief are broadening their definitions of acceptable behavior. With such a wide range of normal variation, when do we begin to worry? When do we suspect our child has stepped over that ambiguous line and needs help?

For the lines *are* ambiguous. Grief itself is an emotional disturbance, and the point at which it becomes pathological is unclear to everyone. Some experts advise that all bereaved children be considered at risk and receive help. Others admit the difficulty of a clear definition and use a lot of qualifiers: *unrelenting* anxiety and guilt, *persistent* hyperactivity and accident proneness, *severe* aggression and destructiveness.

It's an unsatisfying list. We'll probably end up responding according to the resources available to us and according to our own tolerance for anxiety. In an interview, Dr. Phyllis Silverman, co-director of a study on childhood bereavement at Harvard Medical School, advised parents to worry about the same things they would at any other time: "Is the kid sleeping? Is he going out with friends? Is she on drugs and carrying on and acting in inappropriate ways? Kids have to be able to do whatever they need to do except be self-destructive."

If our children's behavior does no harm and "allows one to carry on in a meaningful and reasonable way, then we shouldn't be so concerned with labeling things as pathological," said Dr. Silverman.

At all ages, problematic behavior may follow a period of months or even years of apparent good adjustment. We breathe easier because our child seems to be doing well. When difficulties emerge, perhaps upon the arrival of a stepparent or some other change, we are caught off guard and may not link it to the earlier loss.

The point is not to sit tensely waiting for the blow, or to coddle our children because they've lost their father. We just need to be aware that children will integrate this loss over a long time, and that puzzling or unrelated behavior may still be a response to it.

Changes in lifestyle and routine or even normal, developmental growth may reactivate their feelings of sadness and loss. We have all exceeded our "loss quotient" and, like a saturated sponge, we may have difficulty absorbing any change for a while. "Even good change is stressful," a friend recently reminded me.

And Reba advises: "Don't be embarrassed to ask for help if you have a troubled child. It's better to get help before he destroys you or himself."

Where to Find Help

"Get help," I know, is blithely said and laboriously done—a lot depends on our location, situation, and resources. In searching for a therapist for our family I knew I didn't have the energy to drive five little kids twenty miles every week to a nearby city. That limited us to the services available in our small town.

I'm convinced that the right counseling situation can make an enormous difference; something not-quite-right can be a time-consuming expense. "My children saw two counselors who didn't work out for them," said Anne. "That's one thing I would have done differently. I would have sought out good family counseling. I think that would have helped a lot right from the beginning."

Therapists often have the same unconscious resistance to death and grief as anyone else. Dr. Silverman, studying the records of treatment sessions, noted that therapists would often change the subject when a widow's grief became too raw.[1] "This is a deathphobic society," said Dr. Kalter. "A lot of professionals aren't equipped to deal with it. You need specialized expertise." Finding the right therapist or support group may take some digging. It's like shopping for any other service; if you're not satisfied, keep on shopping.

Teachers and school counselors can be invaluable sources of feedback and support. My younger children's teachers were incredibly helpful and sensitive. A school social worker met regularly with my elementary-aged children. They read books together about parent loss, and each made her own book (a technique called "bibliotherapy"). Eventually they formed a small group of bereaved children from the school.

When my son, "Joe Cool," hit seventh grade, his homeroom teacher was the single shining light amid the general uproar. Mrs. Brown deftly and lovingly dealt with Joe, all the while assuring me how delightful he was. She was his champion and the one finger in the dike for him that year.

Trudy's five-year-old son, Todd, was uncomfortable at the funeral home. He wouldn't go near the casket and hung around the back of the room. When his kindergarten teacher came in, she sat with him and they talked for a while. Soon, Trudy noticed them hand-in-hand going up to see Todd's father. "He was fine after that—he ran all over the funeral home," she said.

Debby would call the school counselor when she couldn't distinguish grief from normal growing-up behavior. "They would say, 'Well, there are a lot of kids doing the same thing right now.' It was helpful just to know the counselor was there if I needed advice."

Just the fact that others are assessing and looking out for our children is tremendously helpful. Any slight shifting of the constant burden of our children's care eases every aspect of our lives.

The Legacy of Loss

As time has passed, I've become aware of how subtly yet invasively life has changed for all my children. They move in their social worlds at a disadvantage. They are different. "I don't know anyone whose father died," said ten-year-old Naomi. We now live in a new community with a stepfather and all the trappings of a normal family, except for this secret, which they share reluctantly. Which new friend do they tell and how do they respond to casual questions from adults such as, "Where's your real father live?"

"I dunno," Esther mumbled. To say her father died immediately throws up that uncomfortable barrier we all know so well.

Our children are sometimes taunted with appalling cruelty about their loss. "Even the kids' best friends would make mean remarks when they got mad," said one widow. "They would say things like, 'Well, at least I still have a dad.'"

Our children represent something so frightening that the only way some children can quell their anxiety is through attack. They forcefully distance themselves from the reality our children symbolize—that anyone can lose a parent. We have met the same denial in adults, but it is more disguised and subtle, not the withering onslaughts our children receive.

As they grow up, some of our children will carry residual vulnerability. Research has identified some "sleeper" effects of childhood bereavement in higher levels of poor health, depression, and suicidal tendencies. Children whose parents died by suicide or homicide are particularly at risk.

Yet, the experience of bereavement may also create unique strengths. Tammi has been told her children are mature for their ages. She said, "Yeah, but they've been through so much more. I think they're more sensitive to people's needs." Because of their loss, our children may become more aware of pain in others, more tolerant of strong emotion, and will certainly have a greater understanding of death and loss.

At a recent funeral of a young man who died in a car accident, my son's friends sought him out for support and guidance. They were confused and unsure how to act and feel. Joe, at least, had had some experience with death. His friends didn't want sympathy or advice; they only wanted him to be there.

"It's never good to lose a parent," said Dr. Silverman. "You would like a child to grow up in a two-parent family.

But if that's not destined to be, the child should be able to grow up and have a good and successful adulthood if there are people around to take care of him. That's a large part of it."

New Roles; New Families

We flounder for a time as our families undergo a metamorphosis. Family dynamics and roles change; parenting styles change. We are unsure of ourselves and feel we've lost some clout with our older kids, especially when they tower over us and there is no strong arm to back us up.

One woman warned her son that she would call the police if he lost control or hit her. She never had to follow up the threat, but confrontation has a threatening edge now. If your will isn't strong enough to control things, your physical strength certainly won't be.

Our families may become battlefields for a time, with the volatile emotions of bereavement igniting uncontrollably. One-fifth of the women in one study said they had become more angry with their children since their spouse's death. We may resent our children's demands and feel burdened and stifled by the constancy of their care. "I became a real yeller," said Debby, "which I'm not at all now." At one point Tammi was seriously afraid someone would hear the family fights and report her to protective services for child abuse.

Some parents reverse roles temporarily or permanently and allow or manipulate their children into taking care of them. Reba hated to discipline her mischievous preschool boys and for a time abdicated her parenting role to her eighteen-year-old daughter. "It was good for me but not for my daughter," she said. The extreme and not unusual example of role reversal is the grown son or daughter who never marries but stays home to care for the widowed mother.

Forming a new, functional family with ourselves securely at the helm is tortuous work. A happy ending is never guaranteed and inadequacy is the gnat buzzing in our ears. For months after Richard's death, I felt the kids' wide eyes and bated breath as they watched me. I was all that kept the circle whole. I was all that maintained the comforting familiarity of their lives. And they knew too well how fragile is that barrier. "Well, I guess we'll be okay," said Joe some time later. It was a slow, cautious release of taut vigilance.

Weak and fearful we may be. We may feel exhausted, depressed, and unsure, but we are our children's last, best hope. We are there. We put dinner on the table, clothes in their drawers. Life goes on, perhaps tentatively, maybe in tears or with anger, but we will survive. That is a tremendous, vital reassurance for our children.

And just because we are consistently there, day in and day out, we may throw the balance toward their lifetime stability. In a study of sixty-five adults who had lost a parent in childhood, those who had become psychiatric casualties were compared with those who had done well in life. The study found that when children lost their father, one great protective factor working in their favor was having a "reality-oriented, strong mother who worked and kept the home intact, instilling strength in her children both through her example and through her expectations of their performance."[2]

Remembering

As our children grow older, they don't forget. Like adopted children, they may someday seek to know their missing parent. They may want to visit the cemetery or create some other memorial. One bride who had lost her father as a child carried two bouquets, one to throw to the wedding party, one to lay on her father's grave.[3]

Some children are possessive of the things associated with their father. "A couple of years ago, my son asked for pictures of his dad," said Anne. "He keeps them by his bed. I had just never thought he might want them, but it was real important to him." Trudy's son was upset when his father's things were given away. Now he has a special box for the things he wants to keep. We also have a "Daddy-box" with pictures and the memorabilia I hoped would capture the spirit of my children's father. It is all they have to know him by.

Just as we will mourn our husband the rest of our lives, so will our children mourn their father. Erna Furman writes, "A parent who was well known and loved will forever be missed to some extent with each new developmental step, be it a new emotional phase or an important event, a period of personal distress or a time of special pleasure to be shared. A parent who was hardly known accompanies the child through life differently but remains as meaningful."[4]

Great Shall Be the Peace of Your Children

My friend, Barbie, is the most buoyant person I know. She lives with enthusiastic, even outrageous, abandon. She buys balloons by the gross; she plays in the mud with her kids and loves the squirmy things that live there. The universe laughs with Barbie and certainly our whole church did when her last baby, Oliver, was born on April Fool's Day.

When she was diagnosed with lymphoma ("Yup, it's the bad kind. Incurable."), it seemed an absurdity. Barbie? Sick? Unimaginable.

"Well, do you want a blonde, brunette, or redhead?" she asked her husband when her hair fell out. She chose the shapeless brown wig during a shopping trip with her children. Its cookie-cutter curls always looked misplaced on Barbie's head. She should have worn firecrackers.

We had a healing service for Barbie and others who were sick in our parish. I sat in the last pew, feeling the weight of living and the burden of being alone. It was about seven months after Richard had died.

I flipped open the Bible. What to read?—something positive and uplifting, maybe Isaiah 55. That has always been one of my favorites: "Come, all you who are thirsty, come to the waters. . . ."

Mind wandering, my eye roved to the passage in the next column, Isaiah 54. And there I found a rose blooming in the searing center of my desert.

> O *afflicted one, storm-battered and unconsoled,*
> *I lay your pavements in carnelians,*
> *and your foundations in sapphires;*
> *I will make your battlements of rubies,*

> *your gates of carbuncles,*
> *and all your walls of precious stones.*
> *All your sons shall be taught by the Lord,*
> *and great shall be the peace of your children.*
> (Isaiah 54:11–13 NAB)

I laid aside my Bible. For many days I couldn't read this promise again. More time passed before I could read it at all without crying. What greater blessing could there be in a lifetime than to see your children established in peace under the tutelage of the Lord?

The children have grown—boisterously, turbulently. But they are growing well, from the sweet naughtiness of the baby to the sassy heebie-jeebies of the teens. Still I hope. And worry. The job is but half-done, Lord.

And Barbie didn't die. "I was healed" is all she said to me.

Moving On

12

The Turning
The process of uncoupling

Grape vines grow beside my house, drench-ing the late autumn with their musty sweetness. After the frost we pick the purple clusters for jam and wine. Their deep hue and scent remind us all winter of sunny days and summer's bounty.

When fruit has fallen and leaves withered, the vines remain, tangled and knotted. It is impossible to know which is being pruned, which branch belongs where, which sprout leads to what.

Marriage is like the twining of two vines. Trained with effort to bend and arch and yield, we grew together until we were twisted and joined, the one indistinguishable from the other. My boundaries were yours; your constant presence bent and formed my habits and beliefs.

A husband's death is like the death of one vine. The familiar supports fail, the firm embrace slips away. Once again we must test each branch and arch—Do I still believe this? Is this habit mine or ours? Some values remain twined forever, others relax and bend in other ways. New growth sprouts, reaching in new directions and seeking new supports.

Some call this process transition; others uncoupling. We feel cautiously about the edges to discover the remnants of ourselves that we still recognize. We begin to reorganize habits and attachments that were part of our role as "wife." We begin to wonder what is next and who we are becoming. Partly curious and often unpleasant, this probing of habits and beliefs is the unavoidable new growth of a living vine.

Life doesn't wait for our recovery but prods us along with daily choices and decisions, restlessly pushing at our new limits. With curiosity and guilt we test what is really ours after all these years. Pam's husband, for example, observed a strict abstinence from alcohol. During their marriage, Pam never drank. She clearly recalls when she decided that this value was no longer hers. With a pang of guilt, she raised her glass and joined in the bridal toast at the wedding she was attending.

Some unbending is a relief, a shrugging off of constriction, but some is a tearful letting go of familiar habits—sitting in a certain pew in church or cleaning house at a particular time in anticipation of our husband's homecoming.

My unbending began with my first trips to the grocery store. I no longer bought Crest toothpaste or Miracle Whip salad dressing, brands from my husband's childhood that he insisted on using. Now I could indulge my Scotch nature and buy the cheap alternatives.

These familiar habits and values were once significant because they bound and nurtured our marriages. Now they lie barren with nothing to sustain them. Nothing encourages or supports the familiar role of wife—the vine is dead. Yet we cling to the clarity and comfort of the role and resist the changes ahead because they are turbulent and unknown. "Widow" is a vacuum, an empty state, an ambiguous role.

Square Pegs

In our culture the young widow falls into a social void. Those who meet us shuffle uncomfortably; they avoid our eyes; they edge away. Suddenly we've become real conversation-stoppers.

Our culture is obsessed with youth and sex; old age is vigorously held at bay with artful clothes and cosmetics, exercise and surgery. And death is a profanity. Widows are living embodiments of what everyone else is trying to forget.

"When a person is born, we rejoice, and when they're married, we jubilate, but when they die, we try to pretend nothing happened," said anthropologist Margaret Mead.

Rites of burial and mourning in our Western culture are brief and ineffective. We don't know how to act or when to stop acting that way. Unlike other times and cultures, no defined ritual guides us; no accepted social niche awaits us. We disappear; we lose status. We try to pretend nothing happened. A young widow in our society has no place.

When our lives change so dramatically, all our relationships are immediately affected. Some relationships are strengthened; others drift apart.

Friends

As widows, our needs are turbulent and ill-defined. Often, they exceed what friendship can provide. When friends say, in all sincerity, "If you need anything just call," they don't understand how difficult it is to pick up the phone.

While some women are able to invite friends over and reach out more assertively, most, like myself, have less energy to initiate contact or ask for help. Yet we need to be connected. We need reassurance that we have a place and are valued for ourselves, not for our husband's position or personality.

But we are difficult to be around with our unpredictable moods and awkward, one-legged stance. We are not happy people, nor are we aglitter with social graces. If our friends are not of hardy stock, they will fade away.

"The change is in me and in them," said Laura. "I feel awkward that I don't have my honey here, and they feel like they need to accommodate me."

No matter how accommodating everyone is, we just don't fit anymore. Our needs and interests are different from those of married people. We still share personal and human interests, but we are no longer involved in the everyday stuff of married life. This is a poignant and painful leavetaking of a sweetly familiar world.

Laura recalls with exasperation a special "night out" to dinner and the opera with six couples—all old friends from "before." From the seating arrangement at the restaurant to the final sprint to the cars in a cozy drizzle, the evening intensified Laura's isolation. Six couples huddled under six umbrellas, wrapped in the afterglow of a special evening. Six wives clinging to their husband's arms—and Laura conspicuous in her aloneness.

Yet, there are the compassionate ones—old friends strong in their flexibility and commitment, and new friends who never knew our husband but come quietly in the kitchen door. One such person appeared the day Reba's husband died, organized the food, and cared for the children. "She stayed until ten that night and made sure I had my bath and got the kids to bed for me." This new friend called Reba every day, listening when she needed to talk. "That was the neatest thing to have someone take that much time out of her own life," Reba said.

"The Lord brought special people into our lives when we needed them, gentle people who said, 'Here, let me do this for you,'" Tammi recalled.

Relatives

Our relatives can be an enormous help. These relationships, however, often contain their twists and toe trippers from the past. We want someone to "take care" of us, yet when our parents try to protect us, we are irritated.

Tammi was determined to make it on her own, so

when her parents began dropping in and even opening her mail, she was "like a cat in a corner: I came out with my claws showing."

Our families want us to get better. So they give us unhelpful advice to that end: get out, date, don't talk about it. "Family and friends lay all these expectations on us," said Marge. "It's not that they're really being hard on us, it's just that they don't know what to do or say. If we're over it, they don't have to worry anymore. It's an overwhelming job for them."

Tragedy can draw families together. We are all grieving the loss of someone important. For our in-laws, the grandchildren are a last link to a loved son. Strained as the relationships may have been, many women forge closer ties with in-laws as they share a common loss.

"My father-in-law used to bring out the argument in me," said Laura. "He's very opinionated. But now we represent what's left of Roger. His folks have expressed so much love to me that it's made me very tender toward them."

We can be tough on those closest to us. It's safe to vent our inner turbulence on them, because they have to stick with us no matter what. Anne's anger burst out in her second year of widowhood, alienating family and friends, who took the blast personally. One friend, however, could absorb it without reacting: "With her I could do or say just about anything," Anne said. One night, however, Anne's emotion was so extreme that her friend finally threw her in the shower.

Like many of the women I interviewed, I have great friends and relatives who stuck by me. They grieved with me while still being sensitive to my need for solitude and independence. Yet, over time I felt a layer of anger cover my relationships like dust. I muttered inwardly that one friend was too suffocating in her concern for me and the other too distant, seeming to avoid me.

Eventually I recognized that I was really angry at my situation and at Richard for creating it. Far healthier for me to admit that I was angry at my husband than to smear it over every other part of life. I also had to accept that the intimacy, the way we are known, in a marriage just can't be filled by friendship. The inner void remains. I had to adjust my expectations and monitor the source and direction of my emotions.

New Friends

However attentive and loyal old friends may be, widows sit home on Friday nights and are excluded by definition from couples' groups. Repeatedly women told me that a significant part of their recovery lay in finding others like themselves. "The support of others in the same situation was probably the single most important thing for me," said Trudy.

Only other widows have weekends free. Only young widows are also parenting bereaved children and feeling insecure and adolescent about their looks. We know the importance of remembering birthdays, and we have the same morbid sense of humor. I had no idea how numerous we were until I began researching this book. We are many, and we are good companions into a new, single life.

"We would push each other into taking risks we

thought it was time for," said Trudy. "We prodded each other to continue, to not get stuck and bogged down."

"Five years after your husband has died, I guarantee you will have an entirely new group of friends," said Mary. "You must find them, and it will be the hardest work you will do."

New Skills

Every step of this new life is hard work. The things that must be learned *now* assault us. We venture by necessity into realms known only to men in greasy coveralls. I have crawled into sump holes to figure out why the ornery pump wasn't working (a sock), replaced light switches while clad from head to toe in nonconducting apparel, and dug out eavestroughs that were sprouting small trees in the leafy mould.

Like most of us, I have bought and sold cars and real estate and myriad smaller items, waded through financial and legal mumbo-jumbo, and indignantly defended myself when I thought I'd been cheated. While I would gladly have avoided (and did for as long as possible) learning some of these skills, I also walk more confidently in the hurly-burly of the world.

And as we emerge from the struggle, we can be proud of the new skills we have acquired, proud of knowing ourselves better, and proud of venturing in directions we had never before considered.

"I usually feel grumbly inside the first time I have to do something," said Laura. "I wonder why somebody doesn't help me. Like trimming the bushes the first time. It was hot and my arms were hurting. No one came, but proud when it was done."

"I've really developed an identity I didn't have before," said Anne, who works with a support group she began for young widows. "I've grown tremendously. I've seen God work in my life."

Marge exudes warmth and competence. Approaching fifty, she has the bearing of a woman at the zenith of her career. But her values and her profession flip-flopped in the years following her husband's death.

Marge was an advertising manager for a mid-sized company when her husband was killed in an auto accident. She was thirty-eight; her son, fifteen. She remembers the suffocating fear when she realized how easily life ends.

Now Marge's office overlooks a parking lot on the second floor of a funeral home. Her salary is one-sixth of its former glory; her days more often filled with pain than power lunches. ("In one morning last week I talked to three young women widowed by suicide," she told me.) Marge is a full-time regional coordinator for the National Widowed Persons Service. She sees life differently now.

"Each day is more valuable because you know it can be cut short very quickly. You find you've got it good compared to others. The grass is often greener on my side."

Alone for six years, Marge is now remarried. "I was at the point with marriage where it was now or never. I was very independent and he was too, because he'd been alone for a long time. Our first six months were sheer joy."

Our uncoupling is a period of turbulence and darkness. A new creation is unfolding—a new person, a new place in the world. We grapple with fundamental, weighty questions. Who am I without my husband? What do I believe now? What will I do with my life? Courage and time are required to answer them.

"Do you think you will ever be able to lay aside your life with Richard and say, 'It's over'?" Dee asked a few months after his death. I didn't know. The question haunted me and became the plumb line against which I measured myself in the days to come.

Laying aside. Letting go. Moving on. That is the work of turning.

13

Woman Alone
Deciding to move on

A*pril 5, 1988.*
Just went to the edge of the cornfield and lay in the warm weeds and sun with the baby. Was driven there, actually, by my troubled mind. I no longer like or want to think about Richard. It's uncomfortable. I realized with chilling truth and clarity that if he stood in front of me I would turn away. Not to reject him but because I would no longer choose that life. I've made it through a year of pain and travail and am at the point of embracing my own life.

Acceptance is still the operative word. To accept now means to lay aside the grief, the incredible pain I so lately felt. To gently "lay up in lavender" the good times, the love, the fullness of what we had.

Acceptance means that, yes, I want male friends. It

means that in my good times I look forward to facing the world alone; in my bad times I'm afraid. However I feel, this is my new life, difficult and dangerous as it looks, and today I'm ready for it.

This journal entry was my emancipation, the final turning. I wanted to move on, not to forget or bury the past but because I was ready for this next, tentative step. I wanted to see what was around the next corner.

As I lay in the warm sun that day, over a year after Richard's death, I knew that this next step was laced with ambiguity. I felt guilty about wanting to move on, to meet other men and leave the pain behind.

For some this is a gradual process, a quiet re-engagement with life. You look back one day and wonder how you got there. For others, the decision to move on is deliberate and may be coupled with a symbolic act such as saying good-bye at the cemetery or taking off the ring.

"You have to make a choice," said Anne. "You will go on; you will give up the grief; you will, in some way, say good-bye."

"I was living in a fantasy world because that's what I wanted," said Reba. "I didn't want to give it up. But after fifteen months I decided to go on. So I took the old soap and water and pulled the wedding ring off and put it in a little jewelry box. Sometimes I take it out and look at it, but I made the commitment to take it off. I am a single person."

Courageous turn into uncharted frontier! Not married, not even widowed, we are single women now, supporting our families, planning our futures. We are terrified or exhilarated depending on the day.

The decision to move on is fraught with fear and

guilt. We don't want to mourn forever, but leaving grief behind seems disloyal. Moving on feels like forgetting. Guilt, unhelpful and unavoidable, will probably hound us. Several women mentioned that they gave themselves permission to let go of the past, explore new interests, and find out what they liked.

We take these steps, but our emotions don't settle obediently into place like cats in the sun. More like prairie mustangs, our emotions will break out again. Anger, sadness, fear, and depression will spiral around. When life is hard we miss the security we once had.

"I'm feeling pretty good right now," said Pam, "and I'm going to take advantage of it." She was visiting nearby universities to begin mapping out her degree program. "I'm learning that I go through cycles of energy and depression and neither last forever."

When timidity and fear race across the prairie, the widow's maxim is: "Fake it 'til you make it." Courage is something we can talk ourselves into. Nothing is as scary up close as it seems from far away, I told myself over and over. And fearsome ogres *did* seem to melt away before my resolute advance.

This final turning even makes us look better. We set goals and begin to work on self-improvement. "A lot of times there's a visible change," said Anne, who has seen many women through this process. "They begin taking better care of themselves. You can see that someone does have a pretty smile after all. It's very exciting to watch."

Married or not, everyone needs to set goals and work on personal growth. Widowhood just casts the same questions with greater intensity, and in first-person singular—what will *I* do with *my* life? At some point we have to ask these questions or we will die on the vine. The choices are clear: Either grasp life again or slowly wither.

I have always been grateful that Richard died in early spring, in tandem with the Holy Week mysteries. While I anticipate that dread anniversary, the earth breaks into resurrection song. Life abounds and is denied with effort. I have too much to experience and contribute to be hobbled by fear and self-absorption.

"Care about something bigger than yourself," counsels Elizabeth Harper Neeld in *Seven Choices.*[1] "It's important to be passionate about something," says Philomen Gates in *Suddenly Alone.* "I see passion as . . . a fervent interest, espousal of a cause that's important to you, enthusiasm for a variety of activities, academic studies—or anything that this great and varied life has to offer."[2]

"When I look back and see the progress I've made, I feel good about myself," said Reba. "The Lord has given me strength. Now I can help someone else out. I don't need help anymore."

The single life brings unexpected pleasures. The reading light can burn late; we can decorate in the colors we like, buy the car we want, and giggle with the girls all evening without confining our man to his room. I enjoyed the company of my sisters, blood and otherwise. I felt more free to have them visit and spend a few days, and I think they were more casual about dropping in. I grew to love the quiet evenings I had to myself after the babies were tucked in. My private ritual was to read, drink tea, and listen to chamber music—maybe a little Mozart or Vivaldi—all by myself.

Being single may not be our chosen lifestyle, and the benefits of independence may not outweigh the intimacy and companionship of a life partner. Still, the women who had come to accept their single state found surprising satisfaction in it.

"I enjoyed the freedom to make my own decisions," said Anne, now remarried after five years of widowhood. "At first they were very hard to make alone, but when I got used to it, I liked it. The last couple years of being single were pretty good years, pretty content."

"I had come to a point in my life where I was really happy," said Trudy. "I really liked being in charge of my life."

Even Tammi, with her four little ones, found that place of equilibrium. "After a few years I said to the kids, 'Hey guys, no man in his right mind would take us on, so this is the family unit. And we're going to make it. We'll do just fine.'

"I was happy where I was. I couldn't set long-term goals—my goals were just to survive, to keep us mentally stable and to take care of ourselves."

Survivors. We have made it—changed and scarred perhaps, but with a new confidence, a new perspective, a more evolved and complete identity because it is ours, not intertwined with another person or a single role.

14

And Then There Are Men
Deciding to date

How do you find a strange man in a crowded restaurant?

Everything had been so cleverly arranged. I would meet this blind date—my first date in fifteen years—at a restaurant in a neighboring town, so no one would recognize me. I would drive alone so I could leave when I wanted to.

"Just for coffee," I insisted to the pleasant voice on the phone.

Never was makeup so artfully applied, nor clothing so carefully chosen—casual but classic, the scarf draped just so . . . the earrings . . . the shoes . . . And all this for coffee!

I drove to the restaurant all aflutter, but a current of

melancholy flowed quietly underneath. I never expected to be in this place—a grown woman with young children dating like a teenager. I was still nursing the baby, for goodness sake! A vague sense of doing something illicit clung like a burr.

"What if he's bald?" I had moaned to my little sister, more skilled in this realm than me. "Or fat?" At mid-life anything is possible.

I turned the final corner and parked the car. I would pretend this was an interview for a story. I would be friendly, interested, confident.

I looked around the restaurant. Nothing.

"There's a gentleman in the other room," the waitress said with a knowing smile.

Male Companionship

Sooner or later we all confront the nettlesome conundrum of relationships with single men. For years our boundaries were clear. Our interactions with men had definite limits that we grew comfortable within. We swore fidelity and tried to cultivate it.

With the death of our husband the contract was fulfilled. Most of us quickly sensed this shift in our position in the world. The boundaries have fallen. Like it or not, possibilities that we laid aside years ago now exist with men.

Most of us avoid those possibilities at first. Another man is the last thing we want to bother with. We wear our rings and slip away from male advances. "The biggest part of me isn't interested in remarriage for a while," said

Laura, widowed for eighteen months. "I haven't met anyone I'm interested in dating, but I'd love to have a good friend to go places with and watch my kids' ballgames with me."

Male companionship is a big chunk of life to lose, both for ourselves and our children. We miss the masculine point of view, conversation, and camaraderie. We miss being admired, touched, valued. "I don't miss the sex," said Tammi. "I miss the hugs." A good male friend, if such a creature can be found or cultivated, goes a long way toward filling some of those gaps.

Bob was my friend. He had lived with us as a teenager and now as a young man stuck by us loyally during our hard times. He blew in regularly with gusts of youthful energy, roughhoused with the boys, and dreamed up his usual outrageous activities. He tackled some of the mechanical breakdowns that had me stymied—the solenoid on our van and the faucet in its thousand pieces.

We talked and argued about everything and sometimes went places together. He had loved Richard, too, and missed him. Our friendship filled a mutual loneliness.

Male Role Models

Most of us fret over the lack of male role models for our children. Who will show our sons and daughters what it means to be a man? How will they learn the push-pull dynamics of a healthy marriage?

"My parents had a wonderful marriage, and I always felt I had a really good example," said Hannah. "Ours kept getting better, and I thought we were setting a good example, too. I worry about my son having to figure out all this male stuff on his own."

Hannah was lucky in that several single men had been family friends since her children were babies. "They take turns doing guy-stuff with my kids. It's been real natural, not phony or forced."

When such easy relationships aren't available, Dr. Neil Kalter of the University of Michigan advises widows not to fabricate them. "I think boys do just fine with their normal, everyday contact with men," he commented. "It's not the mom's job to find men for her boys. She can try to capitalize on natural opportunities, but I wouldn't try to force the kid's interest."

Tammi quietly created such an opportunity by requesting the one male teacher in the school for her fourth-grade son. Although such requests were usually discouraged, everyone recognized the value of this exception. It was a good year for her son.

A New Relationship

In the early months of grieving we want someone to take care of us, to hold us. We need more of a father-protector than a husband-lover. We may seek or fall into relationships to fill that void. However, it is very important that we learn to stand alone before seeking another. Relationships formed by need collapse like a house of cards or grow malformed. They birth much pain.

A new relationship won't be like the first. A new person makes new demands which require energy unavailable in the early time of grief. We would consume a relationship rather than contribute to it. Better to endure alone until that time has passed than be exposed to another load of hurt.

"A lot of people get involved too soon," said Anne. "If it doesn't work out, it's awful for them. They go back to the beginning stages of grieving again."

Even when we are ready to move on we probably *feel* stronger and more stable than we actually *are*. Compared to our mental state just weeks or months ago, we're the very picture of emotional health. But somewhere we know, perhaps vaguely, that our judgment is still faulty and our resilience at low ebb. We are still very sensitive to loss, having so recently lost so much. If a relationship that we have invested in ends, the price will be very high.

"I was involved in a wrong relationship and I knew it was wrong," said one woman. "I was searching for self-worth in other ways. When I finally knew that it was over, I was in the pits. It was the worst depression I'd ever been in."

Worse than after her husband died? "Yes," she said.

We want to be special to someone again; we want to be admired by a man. We want to be valued for ourselves without cosmetics or fancy clothes. When a man comes around and fills some of these gaps, if he is admiring, attentive, and maybe attractive to boot (three deadly A's), we are easily disarmed. We idealize the man and the relationship. We may rationalize that we are more special or more in control or that the relationship is at a higher level of commitment than it is.

Even the most conscientious man can't be expected to understand our vulnerability, especially if we deny it to ourselves. "Vulnerability is like honey," said one longtime bachelor, "it's attractive, but you don't completely know what you're attracted to." Men who are less caring may sense weakness and blatantly try to exploit it.

One way or another, by design or accident, men will enter our lives. How and when that happens is no reflection of our worth. As mature women, we know that we don't "need" a man, but adolescent insecurities throttle us with surprising strength. At some point in our coming-out we become self-conscious and preoccupied by our looks. In the back of our minds we think that we are, once again, only as good as the man we nab. On the one hand we value our independence and may not even feel ready to date; on the other hand we buy new clothes and are suddenly very conscious of who's watching. We begin to play the single-person eye games, darting glances to see if he's looking back. Typically our first glance is third finger, left hand.

Hannah doesn't want to date, but "I'll be going out and trying hard to look nice and wondering why. I guess I just want to know if I did want to date that I'd be able to get someone to ask me out. I feel so contradictory about it."

Sexual Desires

In our relations with men, we are confused. Some-times we want them around; sometimes we don't. But all of us, at some time, are ready for sex. We all have to deal with it—sooner or later we begin chewing on our knuckles. Whatever the dynamics of our sex life in marriage, at least it was available. For me, and for others who were candid about it, sex was a sticky wicket indeed.

After years as wives and mothers, we stumble into the dating landscape as alien beings. We don't know the language, the customs, or the currency. Common sense warns us that sex just to fill a need is a lonely, possibly dangerous, business. Sexual intimacy for us has been part and parcel of a secure, committed relationship. Becoming involved with someone would be a big step for us, and, once done, can't be undone. Physical intimacy immediately puts a relationship at a different level and leaves us emotionally exposed to someone we may not know well enough.

"There is one friend I won't let myself see because I find him real attractive," said one widow. "We can talk for hours on the phone, but when he invited me over for dinner, I panicked. I don't want to put myself in a position where I could be physically tempted and, in a moment of need, end up in bed with somebody. I'd hate to wake up in the morning and think, *Now what do I do?*"

The voices from all sides are contradictory and strident. Just about any flavor of moral scruples can be served up anywhere. Contemporary, secular morality, of course, dismisses traditional beliefs as hopelessly naive or even neurotically repressed. We've all been saturated with this dominant morality; we see it every night on TV.

Church teaching and biblical command inextricably link sex and marriage for good reasons that we believe in. We have taught a Christian morality to our children, and we set the example. The rules for sexual morality haven't changed, but our life has—dramatically.

The women I interviewed dealt with their desires and

frustration as best they could. No approach was wholly satisfactory. One widow consciously tries to sublimate sexual energy in other creative directions. Another seriously dated several men and eventually married the last one. A surprising number of women (including me) dated very little, found someone very quickly with whom things seemed to "click," and got married—also very quickly.

We are in a tough spot with few safe and acceptable options. Probably our best course is to continue living as we always have, "standing in the Light," as a friend said. Then we are assured of living honestly with ourselves, our children, and our God. That alone may take some faith and fortitude and a few ragged knuckles.

I learned three things from my brief foray into the dating jungle. First, matters of the heart (and flesh) can sweep us into realms where we might not choose to go. Second, however we rationalize our actions, we will pay for those inconsistent with our beliefs. The minimum price is guilt, deceit, and hypocrisy. Third, God knows our frame and remembers that we are dust. There is, always, gentleness for mistakes and mercy for sin confessed.

Finding a Man

The "other room" in the restaurant was less crowded and, sure enough, a man was sitting alone at a corner table.

Hm-m-m, not bad, I thought. A little gray. A little thin on top.

Craig had chocolate eyes, fine teeth, and a broad smile. He knew how to use these features well. A flash of gold earring hinted at a rebellious streak, which I have always found attractive.

He was interesting; I was animated. He ordered supper; I drank coffee and nibbled at his meal. He was gentle and humorous; the evening, delightful. We made arrangements to meet again. A light, casual hug and I walked to the car, feeling brown eyes melting my back. I waved breezily and drove away—in the wrong direction.

It's a universal law that you find what you want when you stop looking for it. Contented, vital people who live with integrity are attractive; desperate, lonely people are not. "When you enjoy living alone, then you're ready to get married," said a couselor who teaches remarriage classes for the widowed.

Several women found their present husbands when they learned to be happy where they were. Their time and energy were limited and they didn't need to prove anything. "Men would ask for my phone number and I'd say, 'Oh, why don't you give me yours and I'll call you,'" said Marie. "At this point in my life I know what I'm looking for and I'm not going out just to date."

"I felt very selective about who I would date," said Trudy. "I couldn't be bothered with wasting my time. It was too much hassle getting a baby-sitter and all."

Dating and the Children

Once, years ago, we made decisions as free agents. No more. Our children have upped the ante considerably—anything that affects us quickly ripples down to them. They are open and trusting with adults and hungry for male attention and approval. They have the same sensitivity to loss.

Our children may want a new dad but may be disturbed at seeing their mom physically affectionate with another man. They may be jealous of our absorption with someone else and the attention it takes from them. Their feelings should not determine whether or not we date; however, we should take their needs into account. Opening heart and home to another person is an act of trust, a significant step that should be taken cautiously.

With impressive foresight Hannah pondered the effect that dating might have on her two children. "My children's relationship with their father was very open and loving. I've seen them with my friends. They throw themselves wholeheartedly into a relationship. If I dated somebody more than twice, they would be involved. If it broke off, that would mean another separation for them. What if I went through five or six men to find somebody? In my case, it's not just two of us; it's four people building a relationship, and I would have to pick up the pieces if something went wrong."

Marge underestimated her sixteen-year-old son's attachment to a man she'd dated for some months. She broke off the relationship when her son was on spring break in Florida. "When my son got home he had a present for the guy and was all excited to show it to him. It was more than just *my* relationship. I should have been more careful."

The potential hazards should only be considerations, not major impediments, to seeking another loving relationship with a man. We can be aware of our weakness and potential for being hurt. We can identify our values and limits. We can seek from a position of strength rather than desperation and look in places where men who share our values are more likely to be found, maybe in church rather than the bar. We can buffer our children from initial contact with our dates until we know which way the wind blows.

Or we may decide *not* to look. We may be content with our lives and jealous of our independence. Reba, widowed several years, worked hard for that independence. She trusts the profound touch of God in her life and views marriage as a trade-off.

"I choose not to put myself in a relationship with someone. I don't want to exchange one set of problems for another. I can handle what I have now; it's not always easy, but it's gotten comfortable. I would rather spend my time with my children, visiting my friends, or enjoying my own freedom."

Despite the caveats and cautions, despite the creeps strewn along the way, some stable, loving men are out there. I found one; so did Tammi with her four children. So have many other women. If you want a good man, you will probably find one, but don't be consumed by the search. He will come along when your back is turned, while you're trying to be a good mother and a better person—and probably when your hair's a mess and you left your lipstick at home. As you gain confidence in who you are and where you stand, the dating scene will get easier.

Blessings. Good luck.

15

Father of Waters
God responds to the unanswerable

The springtime sun warmed downtown buildings and city sidewalks. Trees unfurled tender green flags, and the bees courted debutante daffodils, who nodded coyly to the sun.

It was a good day to be alive. I inhaled vitality and freedom. Today I was doubly free—a sitter at home with the babies and a writing assignment just delivered. "Hey, babe, lookin' good," a young pair lounging on a wall called out to me. Maybe it was a cheap compliment, but I was elated. Where else did male admiration come from these days? The world smiled benediction. I had made it.

All the birthdays, anniversaries, and holidays had passed. Once the thought of celebrating these alone had caused me to bolt upright in bed at night, gasping in panic.

But when they came I was usually so frantically busy just making the festivities happen that there was no place for grief.

"I would never do this," my mother-in-law said as we piled into the rickety van for last-minute shopping at the mall on Christmas Eve. It was, of course, a nightmare.

I stumbled with other bleary-eyed parents through the giant toy supermarket late at night. I churned out Christmas cookies during the baby's nap. I leapfrogged school parties and music programs, wrapping and decorating.

Now it was over. The long winter had ended. The holidays were over. I was alive. I had even dated once or twice. I still struggled to keep myself and the house spruced up; my self-confidence was shaky. After some days with the kids I still felt as though the pit of my stomach was dropping out.

But a life alone wasn't looking so barren. I liked making my own decisions unencumbered by another's goals and expectations. New options were open to me. I could choose anything I had the guts and bucks to pursue.

Everything took more energy, of course, since I was prime mover and pack horse. Outings were more work with no one to share the aggravation and long drive home, with every peculiar engine noise signalling disaster.

I rarely felt the cutting edge of sorrow anymore; grief was dull and heavy and visited less often. I was restless and ready to move on. My career goals were mapped out. I wanted a new life to begin—now!

Yet that time had an eggshell quality that I only dimly recognized. I was still emotionally fragile, my life finely balanced. One day could be full of promise, the next sad and lonely, though the same sun shone on both.

I had run hard and fast through this year. Perhaps I would have to retrace some of the ruts I had so quickly bounced over the first time. Perhaps the stubborn questions and the emotions that linger irrationally could only be quieted by time.

Anger has always been my shadow, shielding me from hurt feelings and bearing me into battle. Though I've recognized my scrappy disposition over the years and have tried to temper it, I recently earned the nickname Smaug, after Tolkien's mythic monster. Anger has served me well.

Now anger propelled me forward. I felt dumped, rejected. The child in me drew together its tattered shawl of hurt and huddled in the dark. I denied the hurt. Instead, I would be angry. Even as I missed Richard, I was mad at him. *You're the one who left me. Well, just watch. I can get over you.* I would stride ahead rather than stay mired in the bog of pain and guilt. It was easier to feel angry than guilty.

But the unanswerable "why?" still simmered on a back burner of my mind. I knew the question was futile, but it teased and goaded me. The officer who first came to my house had asked, "Does your husband take risks?" Yes, I nodded with sinking heart and rising dread. I knew his adventurous intensity drove him sometimes into foolhardiness.

Was it carelessness that killed my husband? Was it just an unlucky convergence of time and tide—the wrong place to be at the wrong time? Does a good man die in his prime by chance?

And don't we all take risks? Aren't we all careless

sometimes? We don't die for it. And tragic accidents happen in the most careful lives. Who's in charge here? Who decides when a young man dies?

Predicting the quirks of chance is the business of astrology and tea leaves, palm-reading and crystal balls. So vulnerable to so many deadly forces, we mortals think we can find security in such sciences. If we know what will happen perhaps we can control it.

But I have invested my life in other governances, in a God who tenderly encircles the range of our free will, who works out all things "for the good of those who love him" (Romans 8:28).

Even at the beginning I had a mute conviction of God's compassionate, controlled, indwelling presence over the events. The Spirit of God had moved on the water; a Father-God had welcomed his son.

That was the conviction of my spirit; but in the night, anger demanded "Why?" and again I would roll the cosmic dice: was that death the result of a divine act or of a human flaw? Was it random chance or a sovereign act of God? My questions were never answered; cosmic silence hovered around my doubt.

I knew better anyway. I didn't really expect an answer. I just couldn't help asking.

Father's Day, 1988

By now the cornfield beside our house was swathed in green and fragrant lilac stole the floor. This mid-June season was doubly crossed: this year Richard's birthday fell squarely on Father's Day. Familiar melancholy flowed again as the kids and I prepared for church. A day that had once held a small celebration was now an empty cup of memories.

We filed into a pew located strategically near the door. An active toddler now, Stevie usually lasted less than half the service before I had to take him out. We would wander in the field outside the church, occasionally peeking in on the other four who braved the rest of the service like troopers.

Today the opening hymn, melodic and lovely, was one I'd chosen for Richard's funeral Mass:

> *If you pass through raging waters*
> *in the sea,*
> *you shall not drown.*
> *If you walk amid the burning flames,*
> *you shall not be harmed.*
> *If you stand before the pow'r of hell*
> *and death is at your side,*
> *know that I am with you through it all.*
>
> *Be not afraid.*
> *I go before you always.*
> *Come follow me,*
> *and I will give you rest.*

What a great beginning! I was blinking fast and needed a tissue, which I never have. I always feel so conspicuous dabbing away with a white flag. I prefer the blink-and-sniff method, which this time was barely staunching the flood. Was everyone looking at my red nose and streaming eyes?

Now it was time for the Scripture readings. I waited expectantly, as I did every week, for their proclamation.

With a great hunger I came to worship and frequently the songs, readings, and sermon filled my need. Stevie appeared to be holding out, so I settled back to listen.

The first reading came from the book of Job:

Then the LORD answered Job out of the storm. He said:
"Who shut up the sea behind doors
when it burst forth from the womb,
when I made the clouds its garment
and wrapped it in thick darkness,
when I fixed limits for it
and set its doors and bars in place,
when I said, 'This far you may come and no farther;
here is where your proud waves halt'?"

(38:1, 8–11)

I felt these words to Job soothing the turmoil in my mind. My eyes were filling again as my pastor read from the gospel of Mark:

That day when evening came, he said to his disciples, "Let us go over to the other side." Leaving the crowd behind, they took him along, just as he was, in the boat. There were also other boats with him. A furious squall came up, and the waves broke over the boat, so that it was nearly swamped. Jesus was in the stern, sleeping on a cushion. The disciples woke him and said to him, "Teacher, don't you care if we drown?"

He got up, rebuked the wind and said to the waves, "Quiet! Be still!" Then the wind died down and it was completely calm.

He said to his disciples, "Why are you so afraid? Do you still have no faith?"

They were terrified and asked each other, "Who is this? Even the wind and the waves obey him!" (4:35–41).

Now I needed to leave as badly as Stevie. For the rest of the service I followed my toddler up and down the sidewalk and around the church.

I have taped these Scripture passages in my journal. They are like roses ringing an oasis in the desert. They still surprise me with the clarity of their message. On a day significant only to me, God seemed to answer my impertinent "Why?" from his seat among the stars: "Who shut up the sea behind doors?" And further, with the tender tones of the Son of Man: "Do you still have no faith?"

Once again, for all times and circumstances, for all death and seeming victory of evil, the answer to "Why?" is just "Because." Because God is and because he loves. Faith is mute and reason foolish in the face of the Almighty. The haunting voice of Dame Julian of Norwich, the medieval mystic, drifts through our tears: "All shall be well and all shall be well and all manner of things shall be well."

Still, humanity struggles. Innocents suffer and loved ones die. Still, it seems unfair. I have barely lifted a corner of the depth of human suffering. I only know that somehow, with silent mercy, God dwells in those depths.

16

The Harvest
New life begins

It is 6:00 A.M. For one who blinks like an owl in the morning light, I am strangely wide awake. I toss and turn. No luck. So I stumble to the kitchen for coffee.

Morning hush is all around. Late riser that I am, I always miss the first blush of morning. What a natural time for prayer and blessing the day at its dawning! Cup and Bible in hand, I settle in my favorite chair.

It has been almost two years since Richard's death, two years of desert journeying. Like the Israelites, I have wandered with a glimpse of cloud before me and enough bread for the day.

God is veiled but immediate in the shimmer and hush of the desert. There is no ceiling to prayer. The old walls of unworthiness and guilt, the familiar distractions and rush of time evaporate. There are no walls in the desert. God draws near.

Life is extreme; survival tentative; needs great. Reality shifts like a mirage, and natural law holds its breath. Bread falls from clouds in the morning, and water gushes from rock. Danger lurks in the desert and great, gentle mercy rides on quail's wings in the evening. All who journey in the desert bear its mark.

But for me the pilgrimage was ending, I knew. A new life, unexpected as a rose blooming in barren sand, had already begun. From the beginning of my widowhood I had expected to be alone for some time—five children almost assured my single state—and I had set my mind in that direction. Until I met Craig.

Craig went to seminary when he was twelve. He cut his hair short and tried to please his elders. Then the war began—the war that split the generations, the war that created a moral battle within him.

He did not go to Vietnam, but the cost was high. One by one he jettisoned the fond hopes his family had cherished for their bright, handsome boy: the professional career, the traditional family. Throwing away his own image of the good boy he'd always been, he was arrested for draft evasion.

His hands are small and delicate; he is slim and ascetic with a poet's eyes. He moved to the country and for a dozen years labored to salvage a condemned house, how-to book in one hand, hammer in the other. He dug his basement with a shovel, sixty wheelbarrow loads a day, burying his anger and his dreams. His hands became scarred and rough. Neighbors called him the "hippie on the hill," but his house of fieldstone and barnwood became a shelter for his spirit. He had just finished the house when I met him. I think he was looking for another windmill to joust.

"What do you mean by 'relationship'?" I asked. The word irritated me—so vague and expansive. It could mean anything—or nothing. Although I liked this bachelor with his gentle spirit and quick humor, I could turn down a "nothing" relationship with relief.

"If everything goes right, I mean marriage."

I was stunned. I had seen the man maybe half a dozen times. It had eased me into the exhilarating and scary new world of men and dating. It had been fun, but . . . marriage!

The next months were a torrent of high-flown romance and agonizing indecision. Never before so free and fearless, I could have done anything, gone anywhere. "What about my dreams, Lord? Writing. Travel." I had just begun to enjoy the solitude and emotional space unencumbered by the expectations of even a loved one. Marriage! How mundane. Hardly the heroic image I'd envisioned for myself.

Yet, marriage offered the sweetness of trust and intimacy, the cozy passion of a shared bed, and the satisfying harvest of ripened years. I'd mourned the loss of these; the scar was fresh and tender. Most compelling, five young children needed more than I alone could give. In reality I was far from free. I struggled each day just to meet their physical demands, let alone their emotional needs.

I tossed to and fro for months. Freedom or commitment? Now or later? Was this the right person at the right time, or was I driven by my own need and cloudy judgment? With such a load of responsibility, I couldn't afford to be mistaken.

Neither was Craig the picture of equanimity as he contemplated the total eclipse of his confirmed bachelorhood. "I'm about to marry a woman with five kids," he told cashiers at the grocery store and strangers on the street, a verbal way of pinching himself. We were both dazed at the breakneck pace of such enormous change. We were both too intense to slow it down.

"Close your eyes," he said.

On my finger flashed an enormous diamond in a web of intricately spun silver. It had been his grandmother's from the Jewish side.

I never had a diamond, never wanted one. But this was magic. It sparkled clear and brilliant from its depths. It sang: you are valued; this man cares for you. I was a princess at a tired thirty-five. Who would have thought it?

For better or worse the vows were spoken; the life begun. And still, in the early morning hush, I am wondering how it happened. "I feel right now as though my time of grace is ending," I write in my journal. "To stay so acutely aware of God's presence will take more work and discipline for me now. The plodding toil of salvation resumes, but with the memory of his grace."

Trying to quiet my mind to match the morning, I reach for my Bible to study the passage for next Sunday's service. The first reading was Joshua 5:10–12.

> On the evening of the fourteenth day of the month, while camped at Gilgal on the plains of Jericho, the Israelites celebrated the Passover. The day after the Passover, that very day, they ate some of the produce

of the land: unleavened bread and roasted grain. The manna stopped the day after they ate this food from the land; there was no longer any manna for the Israelites, but that year they ate of the produce of Canaan.

The desert walk had ended. Encamped on the plains of Jericho, the Israelites would till and plant. They would pray for rain and labor in their fields. The special relationship with their God, the constant guidance, the miracles, the daily bread would change forever. Graces necessary for the desert pilgrim would make the farmer fat and lazy.

Like the Israelites, I had been given what was needed for the desert crossing. This was the final rose, a sweet farewell, gathered as the land again rolled lush and green. My desert time had also ended. Back to the plow for me. Planted in fertile ground I would begin again the labor and spiritual discipline of life. I would cultivate the "ordinary" virtues: patience, thoughtfulness, charity—those tedious qualities that create domestic saints.

Still the effect of Richard's death lingers. Whatever effort I expend, "normal" will never be as I remember it. To continue living I must accept, adapt, and create something new. The necessity for such enormous change still resonates throughout my life.

Like skin stretched in childbearing, my emotional resilience has a saggy quality. I hit bottom faster and rebound more slowly. I still cry easily, often in church where the old blink-and-sniff method comes in handy. I'm sometimes caught off-guard by memories, although that former time fades and, increasingly, I can't remember just how things were.

I let the memories go. Scars are covered by new growth. What is left from those many years is the sense of their goodness and worth, the treasure of the children, and the part of me formed there. And knowledge of that unique person—Richard—whom I once knew and loved. Perhaps that is why, after many years of a contented second marriage, a friend says of her first husband: "I still miss him."

I am more sensitive to loss. My possessions are imbued with memory, but things are finite—they break, get lost, wear out. Pieces of my past disappear when these are gone. Once I would have sighed, "Oh, well"; now I clutch and mourn. Another link is lost.

For months I avoided the fact that our old cat would have to be put away. Ivan was the fluffy kitten born at the same time as Joseph, now sixteen. I could never tell which of them was crying those early weeks of their lives. Easygoing and affectionate, the cat traveled through our many migrations and was Joe's buddy, the companion he couldn't sleep without. My son nursed him tenderly as he aged. "See, he's looking pretty good," Joe would say as the ancient animal limped by, gaunt and arthritically misshapen.

When I finally made the dread appointment, I could scarcely drive for weeping and almost broke down in the vet's office. The incident gave me a humbling dose of my own vulnerability. And Joe suffered another loss, made doubly difficult because of his first loss.

This fear and sensitivity hampers the forming of new bonds. Hurt once, I protect myself from being hurt again. I

have paid the price of loss, and I respect it. I kr
human relationships and the vows binding them a

Other remarried women experience the same fear. "I
don't know if I can give 100 percent of me," said Tammi to
her new husband, "because if I lose you, 100 percent of me
is going to hurt."

"I think now if something happened to Brad, I'm not
sure I could go through it again," said Diane.

It's not just death I fear. I'm more aware of creeping
doubts and insecurities and sensitized to small rejections.
Having drained a painful cup, I clamp the lid on tight lest
more is spilled. But I know that relationships and all of life
are diminished by withholding my best. I must let the cup
run free, expecting its replenishment.

So I have work to do in my fields. I cultivate trust that
this new marriage will flourish, faith that these growing
children will mature well, patience with them all—and
with myself. I pray that the rains will come and the harvest
will be bountiful.

Certainly, death has cast its shadow over us. But in
shadow, colors blossom rich and vivid. We are earthbound
creatures, seeking light, yet blinded by its brilliance.
Without shadow, light would consume and even kill us.

Death's shadow casts life in different colors, rare and
precious in their finite glory. I see these subtle, hidden
hues now because of the shadow. "Go deeper," were the
words that echoed through my pilgrim years. Observe,
listen, comprehend. Learn the lessons of the shadow. Of
mortality and love, the faithfulness of God, the unquenchable bounty of life.

Gratitude is a color glowing vivid in the shade. I am
grateful for friends and family and my children, for their

love and support. These are the foundation stones that endure when the house is shaken and upon which a new structure may be built. I am grateful for life and the opportunity still to love, to savor beauty, to create things that matter.

To my fellow valley-walkers and desert-wanderers, to those kissed by shadow, I wish you colors rich and deep. I wish you faith and victory in the struggle. I wish you water from rock to quench your thirst, and bread from clouds to feed you. And I leave for you these roses I found blooming in the desert.

Epilogue

Happily ever after . . . ? Not in this fallible world.

The children and I had been alone almost two years when Craig and I were married on February 14, 1989. Three months later we moved across the state and I was pregnant again.

Julia was our first-year anniversary gift. Lest we neglect this unique medley of our genes, she cried continuously for five months and remains willful and wakeful as ever.

Absorbing so much change has devoured the first years of our fledgling marriage. The process has been very difficult for all of us. Craig has only recently stopped searching for "just a little corner" of his own; he knows it's hopeless. I'm growing accustomed to a new profile beside me and to different needs and expectations. We are learning to solve together the domestic mini-crises that regularly occur.

Yes, I have recovered. I am beginning to recognize myself again. It has taken five years, but predictable tomorrows have finally come. So, the message is the same: life is perennial as the grass. However black the night, the sun always rises in the morning.

APPENDIX A

A Note to the Helpers

How vital is your job! And how difficult. You tread cautiously among the minefield of our emotions run amuck. You must be available and constant without being intrusive. You must acknowledge and deal with your own anxieties about grief and death. You must listen to and absorb our anger, fear, insecurity, and a host of negatives without being overwhelmed. And at some point you may have to very, very gently prod us to move on.

But without the encouragement and support of our friends and relatives, some part of us will not recover. Yet we cannot ask for what we need or even know what it is we need. We may be resentful, lash out, or not respond to attempts to help.

Grief is self-absorbing work. We feel inadequate, overwhelmed, and irritable. Sometimes we are consumed with anger or depression. We are acutely sensitive to feeling awkward and unwanted, so that any perceived rejection is magnified manyfold. We can be prickly indeed, so don't expect reward or swift gratitude.

But our thorny disposition doesn't let you off the hook. You are vitally important to our healing.

Without such sensitive, consistent support from my family and friends, the scars my children and I carry would have been deeper and longer lasting. I also think that because so many responded as they were able, no one person was overtaxed. We were taken care of through the heroic effort of a community rather than an individual.

But a helper's task is precarious as well as vital. I sometimes felt that some of the charity came more from the helper's own need, discomfort, or even curiosity than from real concern about me. People are unique, and support should be tailored to their situation, which will change over time. If you help because you feel guilty or need to "do something" or feel sorry for me, best think again. Your need may not mesh with mine.

I didn't need to "talk about it" as many grieving people do; I needed time and solitude. Fortunately, my close friends made themselves available without pushing me to talk, which would have been a reflection of their own need.

Death makes us all uncomfortable; so do strong emotions. As a society we deny death's inevitability with compulsively youthful vigor. I could see that discomfort and avoidance on the faces of people I would meet. "How are you?" became a dread question. I had to assess how much that person really wanted to know. Generally they just wanted reassurance that I was "fine." I could understand the discomfort. I had been there, too, but how strange and alienating to be standing on the other side of the wall.

Giving advice, encouraging recovery, forcing cheerfulness, and identification ("I know *just* how you feel") top the list of how *not* to respond. These responses all deny the impact of death and distance you from me.

Death is inevitable but not contagious. Coming close to our grief gives you an opportunity to explore your own feelings and anxieties about death and grief. Use this opportunity to expand your understanding and compassion. The closer you come the more you, too, will hurt. Such, I suppose, is the privilege of helping.

Here are some other things for the helpers to remember:

Be there. Go to the funeral or memorial service. Sign the book. But don't go to the house unless you are a close friend or are invited.

Write a personal note. Reminisce; recall an anecdote or special memory about the person who died. I still have all the handwritten cards I received. Your memories may help the young children to come to know their parent.

Send a meal, a loaf of bread, a small gift. But wait a month or two until after the initial deluge. One sweet lady surprised me with a peach pie, still warm from the oven; another with her special lemon bread. The kids loved it.

Call. Close friends should call often and mean it when they ask "How are you?" It's wonderful when acquaintances think of you from time to time with a quick card or call. Remember my cards? They are packed away in a special box my friend Carole brought over for that very purpose. Without being intrusive, Carole would occasionally call or surprise me with some small gift. She always remembered my birthday—a lonely time without the quirky surprises and sappy "To My Loving Wife" cards. On my dresser is a nicely framed picture of the kids draped over Carole's monkey bars—another small remembrance of the time she had us all over for dinner.

Make specific suggestions. "I'd like to take the kids on Friday," instead of "Call me if you need help with the kids." It's very difficult to ask for help or figure out what I need. Press gently but allow me the right to decline. And don't wait for me to call. If I do ask for something, move heaven and earth to accommodate me. It has taken untold courage to pick up the phone.

Mow the lawn. Do car maintenance. Fix the drippy faucet. The ultimate frustration is staring down a jumble of nuts and bolts, utterly unable to make any sense of them. A few, safe men handy with wrench and pliers are an invaluable "bridge" until we learn the ropes and line up our own resources. I'm forever indebted to the great guys who helped me out (and to their wives for not being threatened by it).

Respect our privacy, individuality, and need for independence. Don't be invasive or make assumptions about what we need. We are a *person* you are concerned about, not an opportunity for your charity.

Cooking and cleaning were soothing, mindless chores for me after the funeral, but I sure appreciated the meals sent in after the baby's birth. I'm glad my friends listened to and respected my individual needs.

Invite us over for dinner when the dad is home. "Widows are lunched to death," said Mary Anthony, a WPS coordinator. And we are usually asked over when the husband is away. "I resent being thought of when nothing else is going on," said one widow. And it's good for all of us to remember how two-parent families operate. "Did all the daddies die?" asked one child after many such fatherless visits.

Be careful going on about your wonderful husband or the romantic anniversary weekend you have planned—the Jacuzzi, the special suite, your new negligee (this happened to a friend of mine). It feels to us like you are flaunting, and I suspect it may be another way of denying your own fear of what we represent—that anyone can lose a love anytime.

Let the Spirit guide you. Pray for us and stay open to the winds of the Spirit. Any encouragement is the greater when it comes at just the right time with the fragrance of God about it. My "sweater letter" is a perfect example.

The kids were shocked. I had gone out and spent thirty dollars on a sweater. Yes, I had, with much guilt and no good excuse, spent just that much on a sweater I liked.

The following day a homely, penciled envelope arrived with thirty dollars tucked inside the card and instructions to "use it on something special just for yourself." I've often sent thoughts of gratitude to the anonymous donor for such obedience to the prompting of the Spirit.

However you come, come as yourself. Check your anxiety and discomfort at the door and enter as my friend. You can touch me, look me in the eye, and even mention my husband's name. Keep up with me. So many don't. Pray for me. Let me know you care.

As Nicholas Wolterstorff wrote in *Lament for a Son*: "What I need to hear from you is that you recognize how painful it is. I need to hear from you that you are with me in my desperation. To comfort me, you have to come close. Come sit beside me on my mourning bench."[1]

APPENDIX B

National Groups
for the Widowed

Two national groups exist to serve the widowed. Each has local groups scattered throughout the country. Call their headquarters to find out if there is a group near you. Widowed Persons Service (WPS) operates under the umbrella of the American Association of Retired Persons but serves the widowed of all ages. For information write: Widowed Persons Service, c/o AARP, 1909 K St., N.W., Washington, DC 20049. Or call (202) 728-4370.

THEOS is an acronym for They Help Each Other Spiritually. A spiritually oriented group, its chapters are nationwide. Write: THEOS Foundation, 1301 Clark Bldg., 717 Liberty Ave., Pittsburgh, PA 15222. Or call (412) 471-7779.

APPENDIX C

Suggested Reading

There are many good books by and for widows. Most are directed toward older widows; and, while grief is the same everywhere, a younger widow faces some unique challenges. These books were my favorites, either because of their general excellence or because they addressed the young widow's situation sensibly and hopefully.

DeGuilio, Robert C. *Beyond Widowhood.* New York: Macmillan, 1989.

An unusual and somewhat scholarly book by a young widower who survived the loss of both his wife and one of his three daughters. This book has the most complete list of national and even international support groups and resources for the widowed that I've found. That alone is worth the cost of the book.

Ginsburg, Genevieve. *To Live Again.* Los Angeles: Jeremy P. Tarcher, Inc., 1987.

A warm and sensible book written by a social worker and marriage counselor. Doesn't directly address the needs of the young widowed, but I found it encouraging and helpful.

Lindsay, Rae. *Alone and Surviving.* New York: Walker and Co., 1977.

Somewhat dated but well done.

Neeld, Elizabeth Harper. *Seven Choices.* New York: Clarkson N. Potter, 1990.

Addresses all types of loss. Neeld has read so widely and synthesized so well that her book is interesting and helpful. Also has a very good resource section.

Nudel, Adele Rice. *Starting Over: Help for Young Widows and Widowers.* New York: Dodd, Mead & Co., 1986.

Very good; very encouraging and specifically directed to the difficulties of being widowed young.

Ryan, Joseph A. *Loving Again: Advice on Dating and Remarriage for the Widowed.* Grand Rapids: Zondervan, 1991.

The only book that deals with remarriage for the widowed. Not directed primarily to young widows, but addresses some of the challenges associated with remarriage.

Worden, Mary Jane. *Early Widow.* Downer's Grove, Ill.: Intervarsity Press, 1987.

A first-year journal by a young Christian woman. Clear and personal. I enjoyed it.

Notes

CHAPTER 3: LIKE A BUTTERFLY

1. C.S. Lewis, *The Problem of Pain* (New York: Macmillan Publishing, 1962), 147.

CHAPTER 5: FACING FOREVER

1. Phyllis Silverman, *Widow tc Widow* (New York: Springer Publishing Co., 1986).

CHAPTER 6: LAST DAYS

1. Geri Coppernoll Couchman, "Trying to Live with Suicide," *Newsweek* (October 8, 1990): 12.

CHAPTER 7: LIGHT THROUGH THE CURTAIN

1. "There is a great deal of evidence which links widowhood to an increase in clinical depression, mental illness, physical illness, and mortality from natural and unnatural causes such as suicide." In Margaret S. Wolfgang Stroeve, *Bereavement and Health: The Psychological and Physical Consequences of Partner Loss* (Cambridge: Cambridge University Press, 1987), 124.

2. Elisabeth Kubler-Ross, *On Children and Death* (New York: Macmillan, 1983), 47.

CHAPTER 8: FELLOWSHIP OF LOVE

1. Stephen Levine, *Healing into Life and Death* (New York: Doubleday, 1987), 12.

CHAPTER 9: WHY?

1. Daniel McIntosh, Roxanne Silver, and Camille Wortman, "Social Support for the Bereaved: Recipients' and Providers Perspec-

tives on What Is Helpful," *Journal of Consulting and Clinical Psychology* 54, no. 4 (1986).

CHAPTER 10: DEATH AND THE CHILDREN

1. Silverman, *Widow to Widow*, 94.

2. Phyllis Silverman, "The Impact of Parental Death on College-Age Women," *Psychoanalytic Study of the Child* 21, no. 3 (1979): 395.

3. Beverley Raphael, *The Anatomy of Bereavement* (New York: Basic Books, 1983), 92.

4. "Children are likely to manifest grief-related affects and behavior, on an intermittent basis, for many years after loss occurs; various powerful reactions to the loss normally will be revived, reviewed and worked through repeatedly at successive levels of subsequent development." In Marian Osterweis, Frederic Solomon, and Morris Green, eds., *Bereavement: Reactions, Consequences, and Care* (Washington, D.C.: National Academy Press, 1984), 100.

5. Silverman, "Impact of Death," 397.

6. Raphael, *Anatomy*, 88.

7. Erna Furman, *A Child's Parent Dies* (New Haven: Yale University Press, 1974), 102.

8. Ibid., 9.

CHAPTER 11: FAMILIES IN FLUX

1. Silverman, *Widow to Widow*, 193.

2. Osterweis, Solomon, and Green, eds., *Bereavement*, 123.

3. S. M. Silverman and P. R. Silverman, "Parent-Child Communication in Widowed Families," *American Journal of Psychotherapy* 23, no. 3 (1979): 439.

4. Furman, *A Child's Parent Dies*, 172.

CHAPTER 13: WOMAN ALONE

1. Elizabeth Harper Neeld, *Seven Choices* (New York: Clarkson N. Potter, 1990).

2. Philomen Gates, *Suddenly Alone* (New York: Harper & Row, 1990), 167.

APPENDIX A: A NOTE TO THE HELPERS

1. Nicholas Wolterstorff, *Lament for a Son* (Grand Rapids: Eerdmans, 1987), 34.